D1569029

Ethnic Culinary Herbs

Ethnic Culinary Herbs

A Guide to Identification and Cultivation in Hawai'i

GEORGE W. STAPLES
MICHAEL S. KRISTIANSEN

University of Hawai'i Press
Honolulu

Printed in the United States of America
03 02 01 00 99 5 4 3 2 1

Library of Congress Cataloging-in-Publication Data

Staples, George.
Ethnic culinary herbs : a guide to identification and cultivation in Hawaii / George W. Staples and Michael S. Kristiansen.
p. cm.
Includes bibliographical references.
ISBN 0-8248-2094-0 (cloth : alk. paper)
1. Herbs—Hawaii Identification. 2. Herb gardening—Hawaii.
I. Staples, George W. 1953– . II. Kristiansen, Michael S., 1942– . III. Title.
SB351.H5S69 1999
635'.7'09969—dc21 99-20361
CIP

University of Hawai'i Press books are printed on acid-free paper and meet the guidelines for permanence and durability of the Council on Library Resources.

Printed by The Maple-Vail Manufacturing Group

Contents

Color photographs follow page 44 and page 60

Preface

The idea for this book was born from a sense of frustration over the lack of readily accessible information about exotic herbs grown and used for culinary purposes in the warmer parts of the United States. While the authors live and work in Hawai'i, the most tropical part of the nation, the same herb species encountered here are also to be found in subtropical and warm temperate parts of the mainland—especially southern Florida, Texas, and California—and are increasingly sold in ethnic markets nationwide. As we struggled to learn about the new culinary herbs we encountered in Hawai'i, we decided to assemble what we learned and make it available to others so that their search for information might be less arduous and frustrating than our own.

Some definitions may help define the scope of this guide. According to *Webster's New Collegiate Dictionary*, the word *herb* has more than one definition. The definition familiar to botanists but few others is "an annual, biennial, or perennial [plant] that does not develop persistent woody tissue." Another more widely known definition is "a plant or plant part valued for its medicinal, savory, or aromatic qualities." It is the latter definition that we adopt for our title, and we further restrict ourselves to discussion of savory herbs used in cooking. The word *exotic*, again as defined in *Webster's*, is "introduced from another country: not native to the place where found," and also "strikingly or excitingly different or unusual." Both definitions apply to the plants chosen for inclusion in this handbook because they are not native to Hawai'i or even the United States, and they are certainly different or unusual in comparison to the herbs familiar to most American cooks and gardeners. We also find them exciting—to grow and to use. A brief recap of how we came to make their acquaintance and then to write this book follows.

In 1988, George Staples arrived in Honolulu to head the *In Gardens of Hawai'i* Project at the Bishop Museum. Almost from the first week, public inquiries were received that required identifications of plants growing in yards and gardens. Among these plants were several sorts of leaves and flowers being used as culinary herbs in Honolulu produce markets and ethnic restaurants. George consulted the herbarium collections and library resources of the Bishop Museum and, later, the University of Hawai'i, Mānoa campus. It was soon evident that although there were numerous books dealing with culinary herbs, the great majority dealt with the same few species—mainly of Mediterranean and European origin—that are familiar to every chef and homemaker living in the mainland United States. There was no reliable reference work that covered exotic culinary herbs that fall outside the American mainstream. Hence it should come as no surprise that our efforts to identify herbs being grown and used by the Asian and Pacific peoples living in Hawai'i were repeatedly frustrated by the lack of readily available literature on the subject.

Eventually, recourse to older botanical works and economic botany references from Asia, Africa, and the Americas led to successful identifications of most of these locally grown and used plants. Yet the need for ready access to this information was apparent. It is unlikely that the people who asked us what these herbs were and how they were used would pursue a lengthy search of weighty botanical tomes to satisfy their curiosity. And with the current resurgence of interest in growing and using herbs, many people desire more knowledge about a wider variety of herbs of all types, not just the few commonly used in mainstream American cooking. Thus the stage seems set for a handbook of this type to introduce Americans to culinary herbs that are unfamiliar to them, yet are becoming more readily available all the time.

At approximately the same time (early 1989), Michael Kristiansen arrived in Honolulu and was confronted with similar issues, though from a slightly different perspective. As the newly appointed director of the Honolulu Botanical Gardens, one of whose duties it is to oversee the operation of the Honolulu Community Gardens program, he was faced with a bewildering array of vegetables, herbs, flowers, and ornamentals being grown by gardeners who participate in this urban gardening program. Excited by the many unfamiliar species he encountered in the Community Garden plots, Michael early recognized the opportunity to learn how they were being grown and used, their nutritional value, and their cultural importance to the diverse ethnic groups that live in Honolulu. Having met and compared notes on our mutual frustrations in trying to learn about these unfamiliar herbs, we decided to join forces and work together to share what we found. Having spent several months gathering preliminary information, we decided that a small handbook or manual describing a selected list of the unusual herbs used in Hawai'i would be the best place to start. It was clear that producing the handbook would require further research to gather both published information from the literature and firsthand observations in Hawai'i.

A research proposal was submitted to—and subsequently funded by—the Herb Society of America (HSA) in 1990. These research funds permitted us to: (1) collect voucher specimens for identification and to permanently document the herbs under study; (2) photograph living herbs grown in local gardens; and (3) have a professional botanical illustrator draw the plants in pen and ink for the book. The main venue for our collecting and documentation efforts was the Honolulu Community Gardens Program, operated by the Department of Parks and Recreation of the City and County of Honolulu. The Community Gardens comprise ten sites located around the island of O'ahu; Appendix B lists their locations. The gardeners participating in the program are drawn from all ethnic groups living in Hawai'i, including Chinese, Filipino, Hawaiian, Japanese, Korean, Laotian, Samoan, Thai, Tongan, and Vietnamese, as well as Caucasian. To visit the Community Gardens is an exciting experience, for so many familiar and unfamiliar herbs, vegetables, ornamentals, and flowers are encountered in a single visit that one can easily be overwhelmed by the diversity. We have found the gardeners quite willing to share with us their knowledge of the plants they grow and their methods for using them.

The species selected for coverage in this handbook are all to be found in local gardens in Hawai'i. We have deliberately excluded the common culinary herbs already familiar to most mainland American gardeners and chefs. Our aim is to present a selection of exotic herbs already being grown in Hawai'i—and quite likely on the U.S. mainland as well—so that a wider range of gardeners, herb fanciers, and those interested in ethnic cooking might become familiar with them. The audience for the handbook might also include botanists, students, and anyone curious about plants and their uses. The latter group certainly includes all who wish to learn what people from different ethnic backgrounds might be growing in their gardens and how they use the produce.

We have attempted to provide methods for propagating these herbs that should work well for home gardeners. Our experience has been that many gardeners in the Honolulu Community Gardens Program propagate their herbs by simply inserting cuttings into garden soil or rooting them in a jar of water. While this produces adequate new plants for their needs, there are better ways to propagate that assure a higher success rate and produce more vigorous plants. We tested our ideas about herb propagation with the help of a class of volunteers led by Masa Yamauchi. The volunteers struck cuttings into a variety of sterile rooting media and applied various techniques (hormone powder, misting, bottom heat) to enhance root development. The results were then compared, and the most effective methods are reported here. We believe the little extra effort pays dividends in terms of success with growing these exotic herbs.

A final word concerns the disposition of the materials that document our work. The primary set of voucher specimens has been deposited in the Herbarium Pacificum (BISH) of Bishop Museum, Honolulu, Hawai'i, and duplicate specimens were sent to several taxonomists in other herbaria for expert identifications (see Acknowledgments). The primary set of 35 mm color photographic slides has temporarily been incorporated into the slide collection assembled as part of the *In Gardens of Hawai'i* Project, which will ultimately be deposited in the Bishop Museum Archives. A duplicate set of 35 mm slides has been given to the Herb Society of America.

George W. Staples

Acknowledgments

One incurs countless debts in the course of preparing even a small handbook such as this. Many people have assisted our research and writing. It is our pleasure to acknowledge the following individuals and institutions for their help and information.

One individual has done everything in her power to further the writing of this book, having provided specimens, gathered information and copied articles, introduced us to herb growers, and provided a thoughtful review and constructive criticism of an early draft manuscript to help us along. Alice Kadowaki has earned our sincere admiration and our heartfelt thanks for all that she has contributed to this book and to the herb growers of Hawai'i.

The Herb Society of America (HSA) generously awarded a research grant in 1990 that permitted us to collect, identify, illustrate, photograph, and preserve permanent voucher specimens of selected tropical herbs grown in Hawaiian gardens for culinary use. Officers of the HSA's Research and Education Grant Committee have encouraged us at every step along our way; in particular, Lory Doolittle, Dorothy Spencer, and Arthur Tucker. The Bernice Pauahi Bishop Museum, Department of Botany (now Department of Natural Science), administered these research funds and provided a base from which to work. Kevin Johnson allowed after-hours access to a light table for slide sorting, Gordon Nishida provided references on the mechanism of action for insecticidal soap, while Scott Miller pointed out literature concerned with the Chinese rose beetle in Hawai'i. Katie Anderson capably integrated our two manuscripts into one and provided much editorial assistance in the process. To both organizations and the individuals named we are deeply grateful.

Collecting voucher specimens for identification and, later, fresh material to be illustrated, was facilitated by Katie Anderson, Tommy Boyd, Linda Hee, James Kehrer, Craig Mayeda, Jack Whitlock, and the staff of the H. L. Lyon Arboretum under its then director, Dr. Yoneo Sagawa. Many of the voucher specimens and color photographs were prepared in the ten garden sites that comprise the Honolulu Community Gardens, operated by the Department of Parks and Recreation, City and County of Honolulu. We thank the Community Garden Council officers and the numerous individual gardeners for sharing their plants and their knowledge with us.

Several taxonomic specialists from around the world have kindly obliged us with identifications for the voucher specimens we collected. We thank Miss Sandy Atkins *(Lippia),* Drs. Lynn Bohs (Solanaceae), Lincoln Constance (Apiaceae), Raymond Harley, and Alan Paton (Lamiaceae), Leila Schultz *(Artemisia),* Miss Rosemary Smith (Zingiberaceae), and Dr. Takasi Yamazaki *(Limnophila).*

Acknowledgments

The pen and ink drawings of the herbs were prepared by Susan G. Monden using living material for the greater part, supplemented by some herbarium specimens and photographs in a few cases. We thank Susan for her hard work and dedication to this project. The University of Hawai'i's Department of Botany accepted the loan of herbarium specimens for the illustrations and made them accessible to Susan.

The manuscript itself benefited from the expertise of several people. Inez K. Pai compiled vernacular names in Thai, Laotian, and Vietnamese from published sources for inclusion in the book. Dr. Sabina Swift corrected the Pilipino vernacular names and suggested numerous additions. Ken Nagata shared his knowledge of gingers and their economic and culinary uses with us and allowed us to quote from his as-yet-unpublished account of the gingers that was prepared for the *In Gardens of Hawai'i* Project. And in addition to the review provided by Alice Kadowaki, two other people read early drafts of the text. Dr. William Hoe, botanist with the USDA, and Susan Staples, an avid herb grower in Florida and Tennessee, provided many valuable suggestions for improving the manuscript. Tracy Power provided a thoughtful review of our introduction and suggested improvements to the wording, inducing us to further define our ideas in the process. The final draft of the text was reviewed by Prof. Richard A. Howard and an anonymous reviewer, who suggested further improvements. We thank all these individuals for their encouragement and constructive comments. Any remaining errors or omissions are the responsibility of the authors and not of the reviewers.

Numerous people assisted with horticultural information. Masa Yamauchi and his Tuesday morning class at Foster Botanical Garden propagated the herbs and compiled the data used in this book. Ray Baker of the H. L. Lyon Arboretum provided cuttings from the Lyon Arboretum Herb Garden for our propagation trials. Additional horticultural information was provided by numerous home and commercial herb growers as well as the gardeners who participate in the Community Gardens Program. Nathan Wong, coordinator for the Community Gardens Program, provided plant material, information, and unflagging encouragement. To all of them, we offer sincere thanks for their generosity in sharing their knowledge with us.

How to Use This Book

There are thirty-five species of herbs described and illustrated in the pages that follow. The handbook is organized rather like a field guide. It provides standardized information about each species, categorized in sequential subject headings, with a line drawing for each species. Color photos of the herbs are grouped together in the center of the book. While the line art emphasizes the diagnostic features needed to recognize each species, the color photos depict the habit of whole plants as they appear in garden settings, and selected closeups show foliage, flowers, or fruits as they look in life.

The main entries are arranged alphabetically by the scientific name of the plant. If you know the correct scientific name you can proceed directly to the main entry. The most commonly encountered botanical synonyms have been included to make it easier for people to locate a species that may be better known under an older synonymous name. Vernacular (common) names for each species are listed in several languages, mainly those spoken by people living in Hawai'i. If you know a common name or a scientific name, whether current or not, look it up in the comprehensive index to all names at the back of the handbook. The index will refer you to the main entry under the current scientific name.

If you do not have a name for the herb you are interested in, then the best bet is to "picture-book it" and scan the illustrations for something that looks like the plant in question. We hope that the technical line drawings and photographs, perhaps more so than the verbal descriptions, will assist home herb growers in recognizing and identifying these species. The descriptions have been kept as nontechnical as possible without sacrificing their accuracy, and they should provide confirmatory evidence and size measurements to back up the visual images.

An appendix has been provided that groups the species we have included according to their botanical families; this is primarily for those with a taxonomic bent. It will be clear to those who consult this appendix that no single botanical family contains a preponderance of exotic culinary herbs. Furthermore, these exotic herb families differ from those that contain the majority of culinary herbs familiar to most mainland American gardeners. The exceptions to this generalization are the mint (Lamiaceae) and parsley (Apiaceae) families, so important as sources for savory herbs used in American and European cooking; both are represented in this handbook with exotic species that are less well known. Indeed, it is the fascinating differences between the herbs we encountered in Hawai'i and those we knew from our previous experiences that made writing this book worthwhile.

We have tried to keep the language as nontechnical as possible. Finally, we have compiled a list of the reference works we consulted in preparing this little book and provided annotations to guide readers in finding further information about these fascinating plants.

Soils and Fertilizers

We advocate organic growing methods for the herbs described in this booklet. While many growers in Hawai'i use inorganic (i.e., chemical) fertilizers and pesticides in producing herbs for home consumption and commercial sale, we believe that the short-term benefits of doing so are outweighed by the long-term ecological side effects. Hawai'i is just beginning to experience the consequences of fertilizer runoff and pesticide contamination of groundwater, to name just two serious problems that stem from indiscriminate use of fertilizers and pesticides in agriculture and home gardening. The benefits of organic methods, while less dramatic in the short term, steadily improve the soil fertility over the long term and simultaneously increase productivity without damaging side effects.

Throughout this booklet, we encourage the use of organic humus for growing herbs. Humus is the end product of the decomposition of organic materials; while it may be of either animal or plant origin, the humus used in home gardening typically comes from the breakdown of plant tissues. Decomposing plant tissues produce little or no odor, and humus can be simply produced by home gardeners with a compost pile.

Composting consists of piling up lawn clippings, hedge trimmings, fruit and vegetable scraps from the kitchen, and any other type of nonwoody plant material. When the compost no longer generates any heat, all traces of the original plant material have disappeared, and the product is dark brown to blackish and has a crumbly texture, it is called humus and it is ready to apply to your garden beds and containers.

For those who prefer to buy organic humus, some excellent commercial products are on the market. Sandy soils benefit from addition of Kellogg's Nitrohumus, whereas heavy clayey soils have a different formulation called Amend. Other organic materials that can be purchased for use in growing herbs include composted manures (cattle, pig, or poultry) and sewerage by-products, such as Milorganite and similar composted organic mixtures.

Application of a mulch to the soil surface helps to conserve moisture, deters weeds from getting established, and, as the mulch breaks down, improves soil fertility. Mulch should not be turned into the soil but allowed to break down on the surface. As the old mulch decomposes, a rapid process in the Hawaiian climate, new mulch can be applied.

Where inorganic fertilizer preparations are used on herbs, a few basic points should be borne in mind. A complete fertilizer has all three primary elements needed for plant growth; the fertilizer label will state the proportion of nitrogen (N), phosphorus (P), and potash (K) in the form of a ratio of three numbers. In a balanced fertilizer, all three numbers will be the same, such as 8-8-8 or 14-14-14. Fertilizers with other proportions of N:P:K are formulated for specific purposes. Nitrogen promotes development of leafy green plant tissue, so a high nitrogen fertilizer would be expected to induce vigorous foliage growth. Growers could use a general, all-purpose fertilizer such as a 10-6-4 for leafy herbs such as basil, mint, or thorny coriander. Phosphorus promotes flowering and fruit production, so growers wishing to enhance fruit production of mature chili plants, for example, might apply a 10-30-10 blend. Potash (potassium), the final mineral in the fertilizer, is important to root and stem development; modifying potash proportions has less importance for most of the herbs treated in this booklet. In a few cases, specific inorganic fertilizers have been suggested for individual herbs in the species accounts that follow.

Pests and Diseases and Their Treatment

The organic approach we favor does not rely on using chemical treatments for pest and disease problems. Some general remedies are recommended.

In the organic view of gardening, an ecological balance is established over an extended period of time in which pests and disease-causing organisms may be present, at low levels, and their depredations are tolerated by the gardener. Where an outbreak occurs, simple remedies that do not rely on toxic pesticides may be used to mitigate the pests without totally eradicating them. The gardener must maintain growing conditions that promote optimum health in the plants in order to avoid stresses that lead to disease infection or pest attack. To give one example that is prevalent in Hawai'i with its heavy clay soils and humid, hot climate, poor drainage combined with overwatering is a frequent cause of stress that makes plants highly susceptible to fungal attack. This stress is easily avoided by improving soil drainage and watering judiciously; with these simple precautions the fungal disease problem need never occur. Instead, many people have come to rely on applications of sulfur or commercial fungicide sprays to control the fungus that afflicts their plants. Changing the growing practices would have the same effect, though it may take longer to mitigate the problem.

Among the most common insect pests that attack herbs described in this booklet, we have encountered aphids, scale, whiteflies, mealy bugs, thrips, and spittle bugs among the sucking insects, while leaf miners, katydids, grasshoppers, and Chinese rose beetles are chewing types that are often troublesome. The red spider mite is extremely common. Among the worst pests in the Community Garden plots are slugs and, in some areas, the giant African snail. Here we offer some suggestions for controlling—as opposed to eradicating—these pests.

The external sucking insects and red spider mite can be mitigated by spraying affected plants with a dilute soap solution. In general, 1 tablespoon of dish detergent diluted in a quart of clean water (or ¼ cup per gallon) is a safe ballpark estimate, though gardeners have to experiment to find the right proportion for their particular plants, brand of detergent, and the specific pests involved. This simple and nontoxic remedy is effective because the fatty acids in a weak soap solution disrupt the integrity of cell membranes in the insect or mite's outer body. This causes the cell membranes to leak and the insect or mite soon dehydrates.

Leaf miners, tunneling through the interior of a leaf blade, are not affected by soap sprays. Systemic insecticides, which are taken up internally by the plant, will kill leaf miners, but eating herbs that have systemic insecticide residues in their tissues is not healthy. The only effective treatment is removing all infested leaves as soon as the leaf miner trails appear and destroying the affected parts. A vigorously growing plant will soon replace the lost leaves, and judicious pruning stimulates vigorous new growth.

Chinese rose beetles feed only at night, most actively between sundown and midnight. These beetles avoid light, so locating your herb garden near a street light, backyard spotlight, or the lighted window of a house offers some deterrent to the beetles. Hand removing the beetles at night is quite effective in reducing their numbers. Arm yourself with a flashlight and a deep container or coffee can with a little rubbing alcohol or kerosene in the bottom. Shine the light over the plants and grab by hand any beetles that are feeding on the leaves. Drop the beetles into the can, where the liquid will kill them. The beetles react to the light by flying away within a few seconds, so one must work fast to catch as many as possible before they escape. People with quick reflexes and sharp eyes are excellent at this sort of biocontrol. The same technique works well in daylight for grasshoppers.

Slugs, and to a lesser degree snails, are the bane of many gardeners in Hawai'i. Seedlings of herbs, vegetables, flowers, other ornamentals, and mature plants of many species are likely to be devoured at night when slugs and African land snails *(Achatina fulica)* are present in the garden. Hand removal at night is most effective. Use chopsticks to pick up the slugs and drop them into a deep container (1 quart plastic deli container, milk carton, coffee can). The container may be frozen overnight to dispatch the slugs, then disposed of in the trash or the compost pile the next day. ***Never handle slugs with bare hands; they are known to carry a parasite that can cause a type of meningitis in humans.***

Other options are available, such as dry lime and commercial slug-killing baits in powdered or pelleted forms. A sprinkling of agricultural powdered lime may be placed in a ring around plants requiring protection. The lime has to be reapplied after every rain or watering because it must be dry to remain effective. Keep the lime off the leaves as it will blacken them on contact. Apply baits or lime as a barrier around the perimeter of the planted area so slugs and snails must cross it in order to reach plants inside the bed. Scattering baits or lime among the plants, although often recommended, is not as effective as this barrier method, which also keeps residue from splashing up onto the plants.

Exotic Herbs from A to Z

Allium tuberosum Sprengel

Incorrectly: *Allium odorum*

Liliaceae, the lily family (sometimes Alliaceae, the onion family)

COMMON NAMES: English: Chinese chive, garlic chive; Chinese: *kui choi, gau choi, jiu cai;* Japanese: *nira;* Pilipino: *kuchai;* Thai: *tui chaai;* Vietnamese: *nentau, phi tu.*

DESCRIPTION: Perennial herb arising from elongate bulbs joined on a tough, short rhizome, the outer sheath fibrous and netted. Leaves 4–9, linear, flat (not cylindrical), 6–16 inches × 0.12–0.25 inch, solid (not hollow), keeled on the back side, with a strong garlic odor when bruised. Inflorescence scape 12–20 inches tall, umbel many-flowered, 1.5–2 inches across, pedicels 2–3 times as long as flowers; flowers star shaped, fragrant, petals white with green or brownish midvein; filaments free, slightly shorter than or equal to length of petals. Fruit obovate, broader at the apex.

DISTRIBUTION: Native to Southeast Asia and widely cultivated in other parts of Asia (e.g., China), which seems to be how it came by its English common name.

USE: Unlike garlic, the bulb is never eaten, only the leaves and inflorescence stalks. The leaves impart a honeyed sweetness as well as a garlic flavor to salads, soups, noodles, and meat dumpling fillings, or they may be parboiled as a vegetable. Both fresh, dark green leaves and etiolated yellowish leaves that have been grown in the dark are used. This species flowers from August to October, and the stalks with buds are harvested as well as the leaves. The scapes with buds still contained in the papery sheath are harvested and eaten stir-fried with beef or seafood, braised with bean curd, or stir-fried alone as a side dish. Individual flowers are added to salads.

EXPOSURE: Plants grow best in full sun or partial (light) shade.

PROPAGATION METHODS:

Seed: Easily grown from seed, but this is time consuming.

Cuttings: Cannot be propagated by cuttings.

Division: The easiest form of propagation. When clumps have developed to 4–6 inches in diameter, dig up and divide into clusters of three to five plants, cut back the top growth to ca. 2–3 inches, and replant divisions into enriched soil.

CULTURAL PRACTICES: Plant divisions 6 inches apart in full sun, preferably in well-drained soil, although garlic chives will survive in poor soil conditions. After flowering the entire plant can be cut to the ground, which will stimulate new

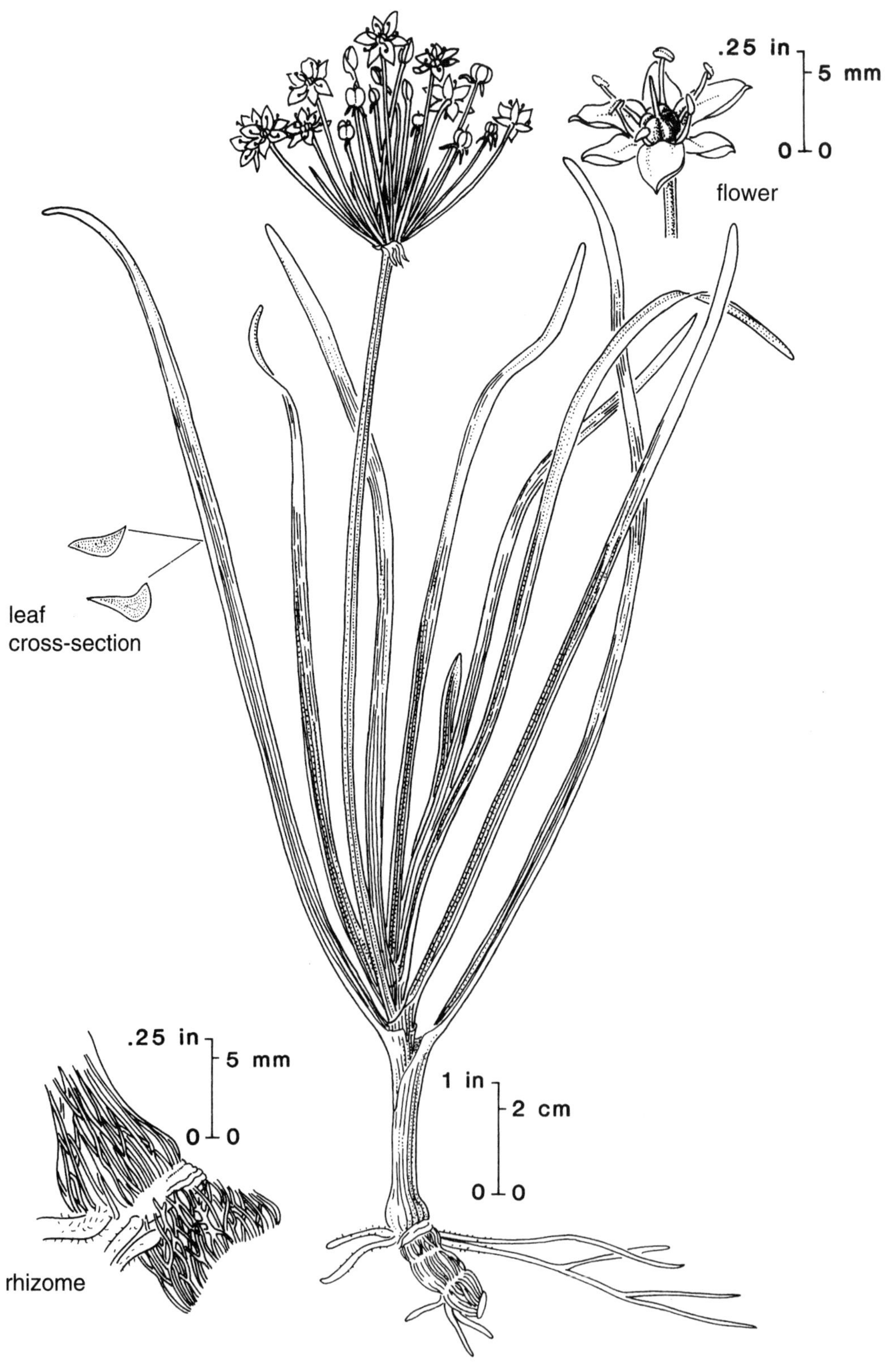

Allium tuberosum

growth, or just the flower stalks pulled out. The plants are evergreen and attractive as long as old flower heads are removed. Garlic chive has many uses, and it can therefore be planted in large numbers in rows or groups. It is an excellent companion plant to grow with roses and plants that are susceptible to aphids.

PESTS: Garlic chives can sometimes become infested with a minute black aphid, which can be removed by spraying with 1 tablespoon of liquid dish detergent in 1 gallon of water. Leaf miners tend to become a problem and it is recommended that affected leaves (1) be removed and destroyed or (2) sprayed with Sevin if the leaves are not to be eaten.

COMMENTS: Fast growing.

Alpinia galanga (Linnaeus) Willdenow
Zingiberaceae, the ginger family

COMMON NAMES: English: galanga, greater galanga, *laos,* Siamese ginger; Thai: *kha, khaa;* Vietnamese: *rieng, gieng.*

DESCRIPTION: Deciduous perennial herb 4–7 feet tall, proliferating from underground rhizomes. Stems with leaves in two ranks; blades oblong to lanceolate, 10–24 inches × 2–6 inches, minutely hairy on the underside or glabrous. Inflorescence terminal on the leafy shoot, a panicle 7–15 inches long, the axis densely velvety; lower 2–3 bracts narrow, 2–6 inches long, persistent, the upper bracts deciduous. Flowers in clusters of 2–5, greenish white, the labellum often parted at the apex, white with oblique red veins. Fruit a globose capsule about 0.33 inch in diameter.

DISTRIBUTION: The precise natural distribution for galanga is unknown as it has been cultivated since ancient times. It is now widely distributed in India, Myanmar, Southeast Asia, Malaysia, and Indonesia.

USE: The rhizome is used—either fresh when young or dried (sliced or powdered)—to flavor soups, curries, stews, and sauces throughout the regions listed above. One popular Thai soup, *tom kha gai,* combines chicken, coconut milk, fresh or dried galanga, fresh lemon grass, and other seasonings in a delicious and hearty dish that derives its unique flavor from the musty aroma of galanga. In Java the rhizome is used to flavor bean curd and in India and Russia to flavor alcoholic beverages. In Malaysia the fruits are sometimes substituted for cardamom and the flowers are occasionally eaten in salads. The medicinal uses for the plant are numerous and it has been recorded as an important part of many pharmacopeiae since AD 600.

EXPOSURE: Like most gingers, galanga requires a sheltered situation in order to thrive. Partial sunlight is suitable and protection from winds is essential. Large specimen plants will develop under ideal conditions.

PROPAGATION METHODS:

Seed: Not usually done.

Cuttings: Not usually done.

Division: When the plants are dormant, the rhizomes can be divided and replanted. Once established, the rhizomes proliferate readily.

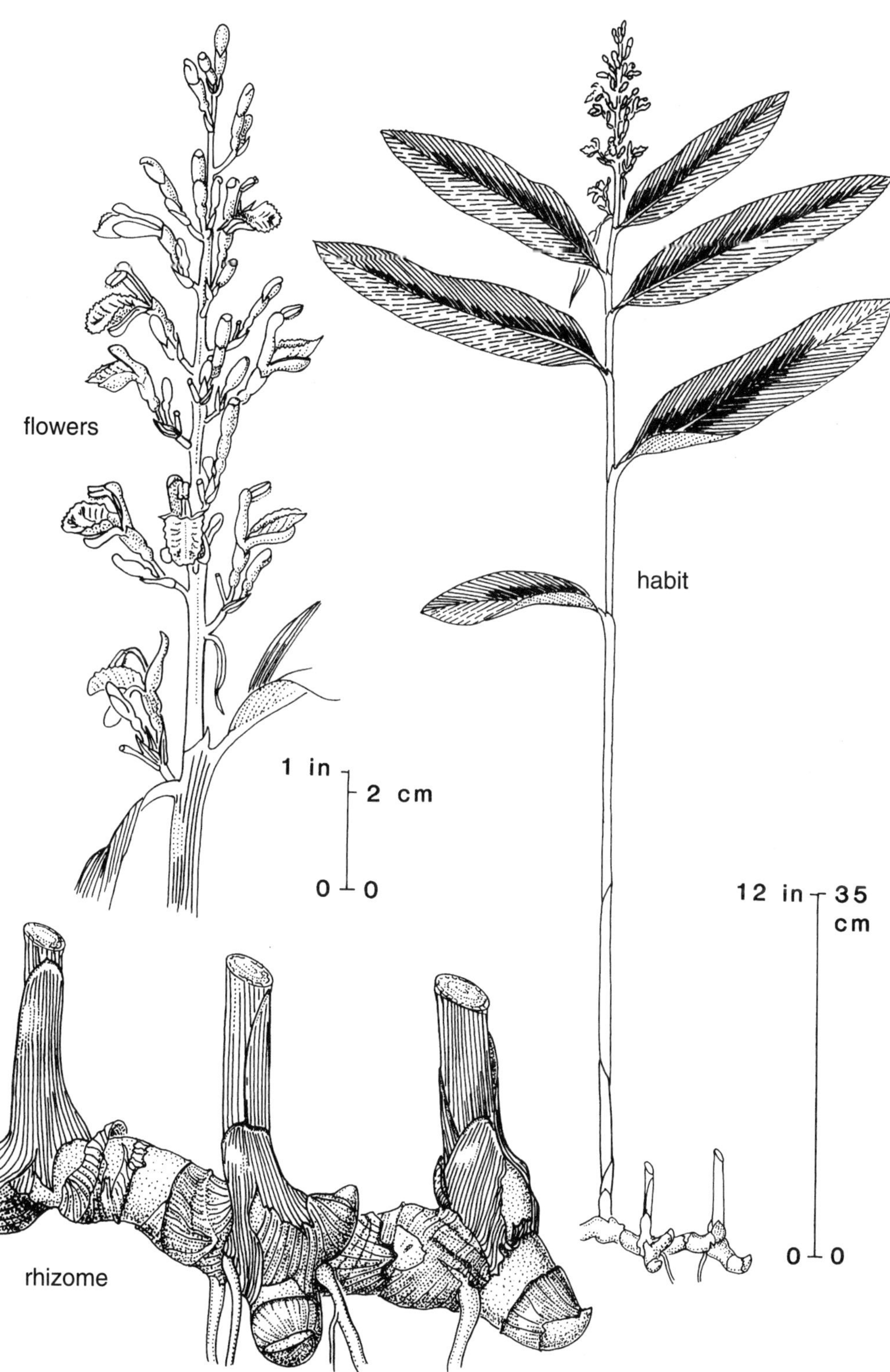

Alpinia galanga

CULTURAL PRACTICES: Plant in an organically rich, well-drained soil. During the active growing season, water must be amply supplied; watering should be reduced in the dormant season to prevent rotting of the rhizomes. The rhizomes can be lifted with a spading fork, divided, and planted 24 inches apart. The soil should be dug to a depth of 12 inches and mixed with one-third humus. After planting the rhizomes 6 inches deep, water thoroughly. Once the plant is growing vigorously, water regularly but do not allow the soil to become soggy. The frequency and amount of water should be increased as the plant matures. Inadequate water and exposure to wind cause brown leaf margins, after which the leaf dies.

PESTS: None have been noticed.

COMMENTS: Fast growing.

Artemisia vulgaris Linnaeus

Asteraceae (or Compositae), the daisy family

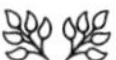

COMMON NAMES: English: mugwort; Chinese: *ngaai, ai;* Japanese: *yomogi;* Pilipino: *arbaaka, damong-maria, tinisas.*

DESCRIPTION: Perennial herb with creeping underground stolons and fibrous roots. Stems usually about 12–24 inches tall, tufted from the stolons, branched, often whitish cobwebby hairy. Leaves appearing stipulate at the base, lower to middle leaves with blade elliptic in outline, 2–4.5 inches × 1.5–3 inches, pinnately lobed or divided into 2–4 pairs of segments, these toothed or deeply incised or rarely entire, upper side deep green, underside silvery whitish hairy; upper leaves becoming smaller, usually 3-parted or -lobed, the lobes entire. Inflorescence a terminal panicle of crowded racemes, the heads ca. 0.1 inch long, the florets brownish. Fruits minute achenes.

DISTRIBUTION: *Artemisia vulgaris* is widely distributed in Eurasia and is sparingly naturalized as a weed as well as cultivated in Hawai'i. Closely related and difficult to distinguish from it, *Artemisia princeps* Pampanini is native to Japan (Honshu, Kyushu, and Shikoku), the Bonin (Ogasawara) Islands, and Korea where it is common in waste ground and thickets at low elevations. Botanically, the two species are so similar that even a specialist confuses them. In fact, both so-called species may belong to one highly variable and widely distributed north temperate species. Both scientific names are used for plants grown in Hawai'i. Plants called *yomogi* are used as culinary herbs, most often by people of Japanese and Okinawan descent living in Hawai'i.

USE: After the bitterness has been removed by blanching or boiling, the young fresh leaves are used in soups and salads. They also freeze well. A special kind of rice cake *(mochi)* is prepared from *yomogi* at New Year: The leaves are pounded with cooked glutinous rice to create a product with a distinctive flavor and scent and a moss green color.

EXPOSURE: Grown in full sun or partial shade. *Yomogi* is best grown in full sun to promote a compact, bushy habit that is more attractive.

PROPAGATION METHODS:

Seed: Not used locally.

Cuttings: May be propagated by 5-inch long, slightly woody tip cuttings, though this is rarely done in Hawai'i. The tips should be cleanly cut below the node, with all lower leaves carefully removed, and the cuttings inserted in either pure peat moss or a

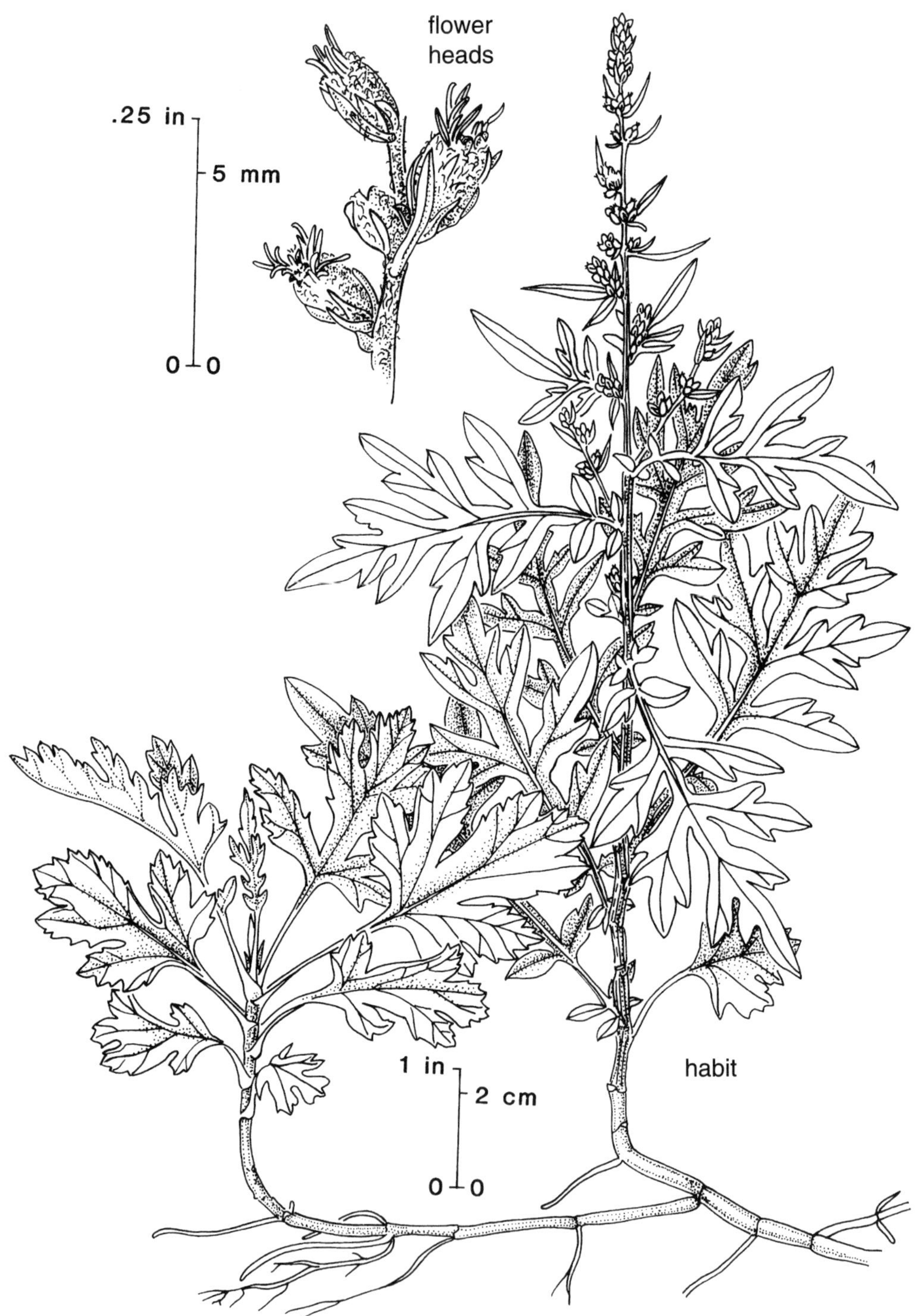

Artemisia vulgaris

50:50 peat-perlite mixture. With bottom heat, strong roots form in fourteen days; without bottom heat, roots strike in twenty-one days but are not as well developed.

Division: Often propagated vegetatively by dividing clumps of plants; the underground stolons readily strike root when separated and replanted. *Yomogi* can become invasive and will spread aggressively from the area where planted to other parts of the garden.

CULTURAL PRACTICES: This plant can become invasive, and growing *yomogi* in a container will prevent its invading other plantings. At the end of the growing season the clump should be cut back severely and older portions discarded.

PESTS: None have been noticed.

COMMENTS: Growth is rapid and aggressive. Establishes itself within the first season.

Boesenbergia rotunda (Linnaeus) Mansfield
Zingiberaceae, the ginger family

COMMON NAMES: English: Chinese key (alluding to the resemblance of the roots to an old-fashioned key used in China); Thai: *khachai, krachai.*

DESCRIPTION: Deciduous perennial herb ca. 20 inches tall, proliferating from underground rhizomes; roots cylindrical, tapering, succulent, canary yellow inside. Leaves 1–6, basal, in 2 ranks, erect; blade broadly elliptic, ca. 10 inches × 4–5 inches. Inflorescence terminal on the leafy shoot, barely visible among the leaves, slightly compressed; bracts in 2 ranks, each subtending a single flower. Flowers protruding from the bracts, the uppermost opening first; labellum petal bilobed, somewhat ruffled, deep pink becoming rose purple at the base. Fruit a dehiscent capsule, crowned by the persistent calyx.

DISTRIBUTION: Chinese key is cultivated throughout India, Southeast Asia, and Malaysia and is probably native somewhere in that region, although the precise place of origin is unknown.

USE: When mature, Chinese key develops 6- to 8-inch-long thickened roots that have a pleasant fragrance and flavor. These roots are slightly thicker than a pencil and yellow inside. The rhizome and roots are used fresh or dried to add a spicy, aromatic flavor to food. The rhizomes also have numerous medicinal uses.

EXPOSURE: Like most gingers, Chinese key requires a sheltered situation to thrive and look its best; partial sunlight is desirable and protection from drying winds is a must. Because the leaves are delicate and broad, they tend to dry along the margins and tear if exposed to wind, resulting in an ugly plant, particularly if it has insufficient moisture.

PROPAGATION METHODS:

Seed: Not known.

Cuttings: The rhizomes, which are modified stems, are separated and cut into 4- to 6-inch lengths as cuttings. All root growth and soil particles are removed. Clean cuts are made through the rhizome before inserting horizontally for propagation.

Division: This plant is most easily grown by division. At the end of the growing season when the plant has become dormant (December), the rhizomes can be dug up with a spading fork and divided for replanting.

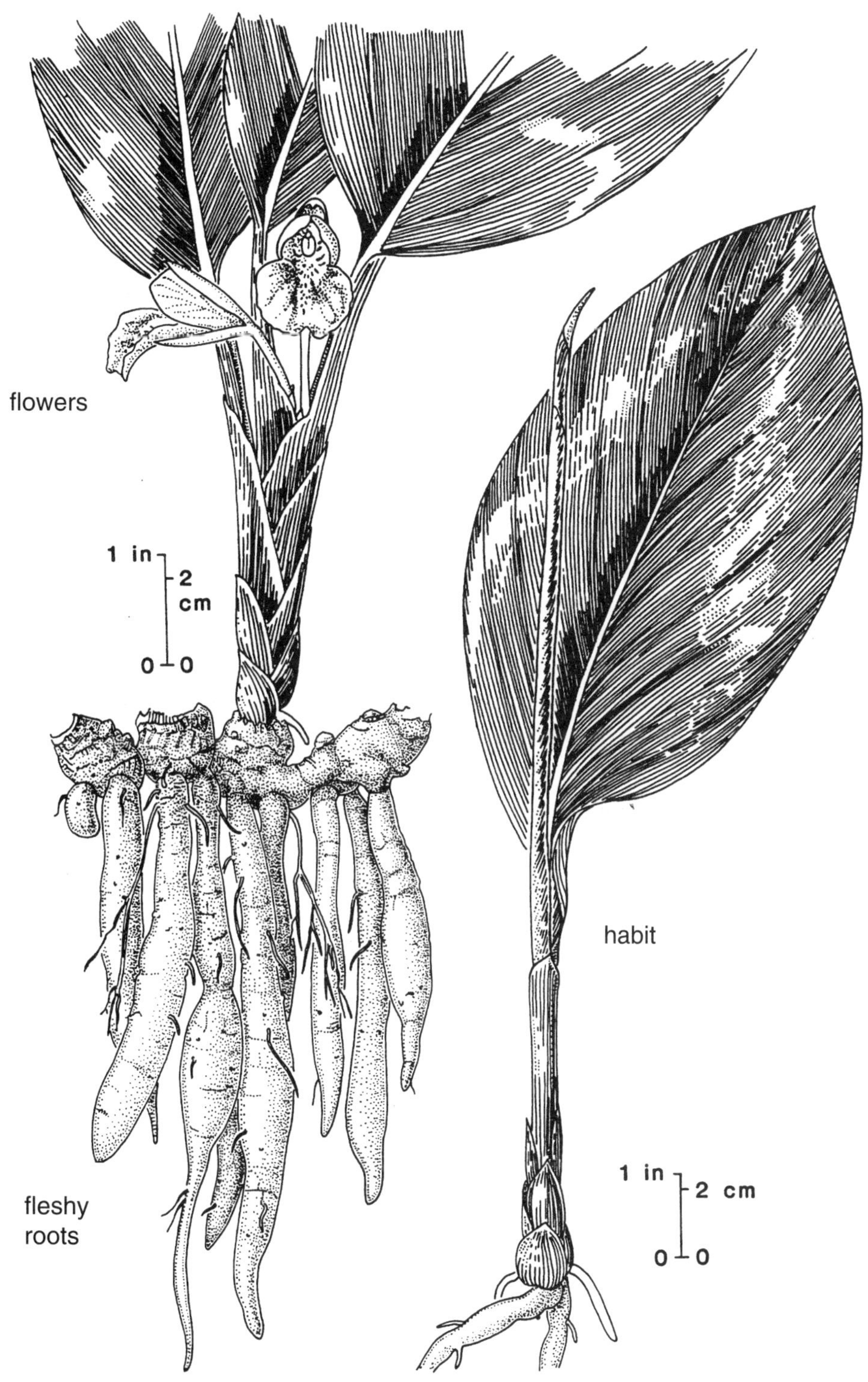

Boesenbergia rotunda

CULTURAL PRACTICES: Plant in an organically rich, well-drained soil. The plants are deciduous in winter and become dormant; watering should be reduced at this stage. When all the leaves have died down the rhizomes can be forked up, divided, and replanted 24 inches apart. The soil should be dug to a depth of 12 inches and enriched with one-third humus. After planting the rhizomes ½ to 1 inch deep, water thoroughly and do not water again until new shoots emerge from the soil. Once the plant is growing vigorously, water regularly but do not allow the soil to become soggy. The frequency and amount of water need to be increased as the leaves mature. If the plant tends to dry out due to inadequate water supply or wind exposure, the browning along the leaf margins will increase.

PESTS: None have been noticed.

COMMENTS: Rapidly develops into a mature plant (within one season).

Capsicum annuum Linnaeus

Synonym: *Capsicum frutescens* Linnaeus, *C. chinense* Jacquin

Capsicum baccatum Linnaeus

Synonym: *Capsicum pendulum* Willdenow

Solanaceae, the potato family

COMMON NAMES: English: chili pepper; Chinese: *laat jiu, tseng jiu;* Japanese: *karashi;* Okinawan: *kōrēgusu, tōgarashi;* Pilipino: *sili, siling pasite;* Thai: *phrik chee fa, phrik ee nu;* Vietnamese: *ot, ot tau, cai ot, lat tsiao.*

DESCRIPTION: *Capsicum annuum* is a perennial up to 5 feet tall with a semi-woody stem base. Leaves alternate, simple, blade entire, ovate to elliptic, base truncate or tapered into the petiole, apex pointed. Single to several flowers per leaf axil; calyx entire or usually with 5 (up to 6–8) short teeth; corolla milky white or greenish white (sometimes purplish), usually 5- (up to 6- to 8-) lobed, without any spots inside at base of lobes; anthers blue to purple before opening to release pollen. Fruit erect or pendent, extremely variable in shape, size, color, and pungency.

Capsicum baccatum differs in having flowers with a long-toothed calyx, usually a 6- to 8-lobed corolla having yellowish blotches on the basal area of the lobes, and anthers that are whitish before they open to shed their pollen. The fruits tend to be pendent and milder in flavor than hot forms of *C. annuum.*

DISTRIBUTION: Native to tropical America, where *Capsicum* species were domesticated long before the first Europeans arrived. They were certainly widely distributed by humans throughout the American tropics before documented history, so the precise country of origin is unknown.

USE: Hot chili peppers are used as flavoring in Southeast Asian, Chinese, Korean, and Indian cuisines, as well as in many African and Latin American foods. They are almost ubiquitous in the ethnic foods of Hawai‘i; even Japanese and many Pacific Islanders have recently adopted them. The fruits are used—fresh or dried—in sauces, curries, salad dressings, vinegar waters, as a stir-fry component, and in marinades, soups, and condiments. The whitish flesh of the placenta that bears the seeds is the hottest part of the fruit, containing a much greater concentration of the chemical capsaicin than does the fruit wall. The placenta and seeds are sometimes removed if a milder dish is desired. Kimchi is a type of Korean pickled vegetable that relies heavily on chilies and often garlic for flavor. Thai food also requires large proportions of spicy chilies for many dishes. Serving a bottle of chili pepper water is a common practice on Thai and Filipino dining tables.

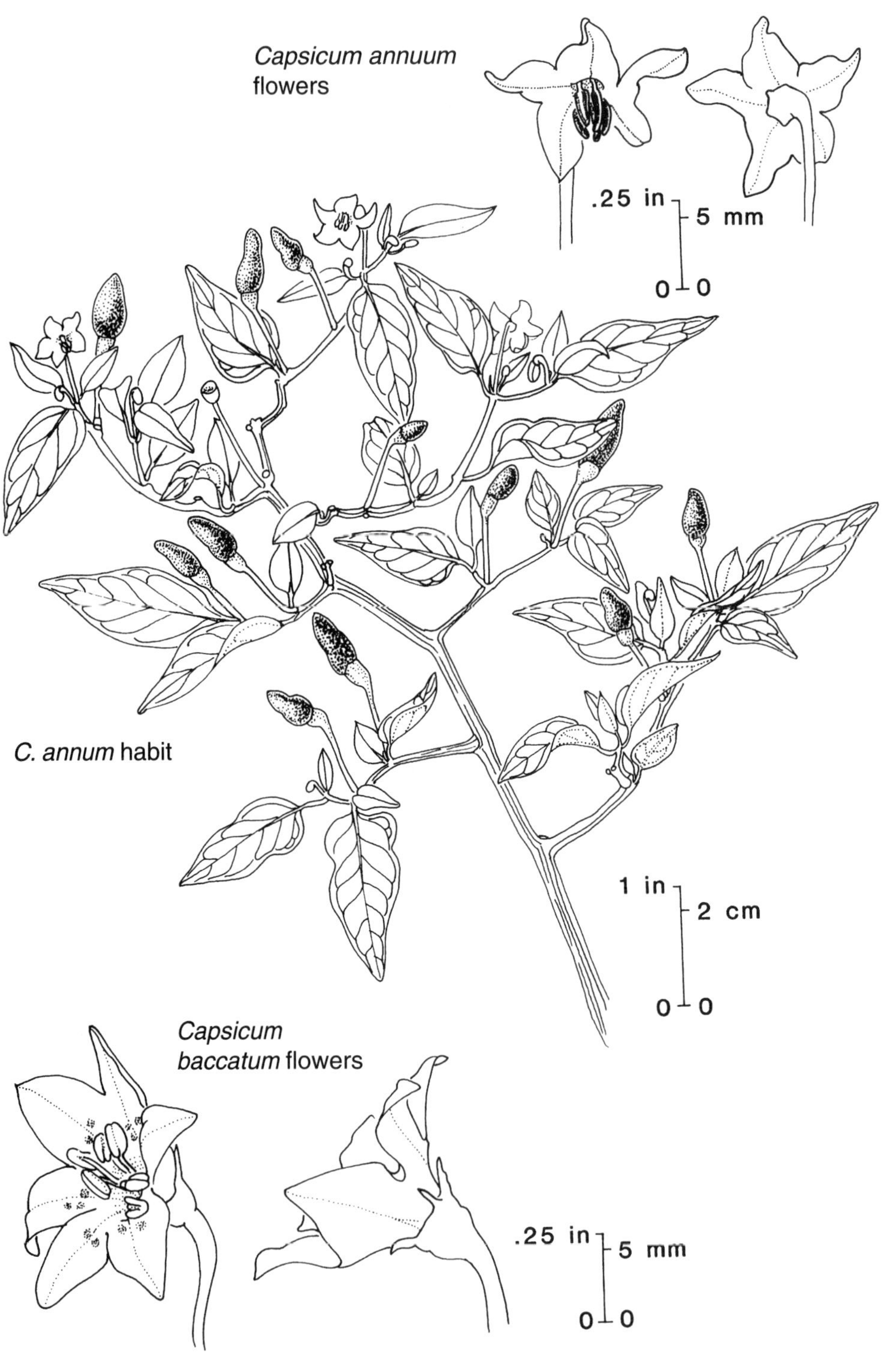
Capsicum annuum
flowers
.25 in
5 mm
0
0
C. annum habit
1 in
2 cm
0
0
Capsicum
baccatum flowers
.25 in
5 mm
0
0

Capsicum

EXPOSURE: Full sun. Plants grown in partial shade do not bear as well.

PROPAGATION METHODS:

Seed: Chilies are easily and most often propagated from seed, either that saved from garden-grown plants or purchased from a store or catalog. Seed is sown in 18-inch square trays or pans in garden soil or potting soil and watered with a fine sprinkling head. The seed is thinly covered with the soil. Some gardeners prefer to purchase seedlings from a nursery. Do not let the soil dry out completely, and when germination occurs watch out for damping-off—sudden death of seedlings from fungal disease fostered by high humidity and poor air circulation.

Cuttings: Chili peppers are easily started from 3- to 4-inch tip cuttings; this method is sometimes used by gardeners wishing to maintain a specific stock that may not come true from seed. The cuttings are inserted in either pure peat moss or a 50:50 peat-perlite medium over bottom heat. With bottom heat, good root formation takes place in seven to fourteen days; an additional seven days are beneficial to root maturity before transplanting is attempted. Without bottom heat, root formation is inferior and the cuttings develop much more slowly.

Division: Not applicable.

CULTURAL PRACTICES: Seedlings germinated indoors in a protected environment are planted outdoors after being gradually acclimated to ambient outdoor conditions—a process known as hardening off. They should be spaced 12 to 24 inches apart in rows or in groups in full sun. Chilies require regular watering; if they dry out, frequently the lower leaves are shed and dry twigs develop, producing an ugly and less productive plant. As the plant develops, pinching out the central growth stimulates side branches, which enhances the chili crop. In a subtropical climate the annual chilies will grow for more than one season, but their productivity tends to diminish unless pruned and fertilized. After harvesting the first crop, all dead twigs and scraggly growth should be cut back to the next lower healthy node and organic fertilizer applied. This can lead to bountiful successive crops. Chilies can be higher maintenance plants when grown as perennials. Plants are most productive when grown as annuals.

PESTS: Plants are often found to be infested by sucking insects, especially aphids and whiteflies; these may be treated by spraying with 1 tablespoon of dishwashing detergent in 1 quart of water and repeated as often as necessary. Bulbuls will damage or eat the fruits as they begin to turn red, and it is necessary to drape the plants with bird netting or place some moving object (such as a windmill, fluttering flags, streamers, aluminum pie plates hung from a string, etc.) near them to scare away these avian nuisances.

COMMENTS: Growth is very rapid, producing chilies within the first growing season.

Chrysanthemum coronarium Linnaeus

Asteraceae (or Compositae), the daisy family

COMMON NAMES: English: garland chrysanthemum, edible chrysanthemum, chop suey greens; Chinese: *tong ho, tung ho choi, tung hao;* Japanese: *shingiku, shungiku;* Korean: *ssukkat;* Okinawan: *shunchiku;* Pilipino: *tango;* Thai: *phak tango;* Vietnamese: *tan o, rau cuc, can o.*

DESCRIPTION: Plants up to 3 feet tall (when flowering), stems fibrous and tough. Leaves spirally arranged, dense near base of plant, becoming more widely spaced as the stems elongate, blade shallowly divided, 3–5 inches long and 1.5–2 inches wide, the lobes ± pointed to blunt, with toothed and cut margins, light green and slightly leathery, succulent textured; the upper leaves are more deeply toothed and divided. Flower heads yellow, resembling small chrysanthemums, developing in terminal corymbs (flat-topped clusters) on the stems.

DISTRIBUTION: Garland chrysanthemum occurs in the wild in the Mediterranean region. Cultivated plants have been classified in three cultivar groups; the edible sort is favored by many Asian peoples, who like the somewhat resinous flavor. Western gardeners grow a different variety strictly for ornamental purposes. Since at least Roman times, the flowers were twined into garlands to wear on the head and around the neck—hence the common name.

USE: Only young plants less than 12 inches in height are eaten. They are used in many ways in the cuisines of Asia: The fresh leaves are used to flavor soups or a traditional "hot pot" by the Cantonese, as well as in mixed stir-fry dishes; the outer (ray) flowers to garnish snake meat dishes (!); and the leaves and young stems as a vegetable by the Hunanese and the Vietnamese. In Hawai'i, the edible chrysanthemum is often seen at New Year's time and seems to be a part of traditional holiday dishes prepared specially for that season. Chrysanthemum greens are plentiful in Hawai'i during the winter months and are an integral component of lunar new year specialty dishes among several Asian ethnic groups.

EXPOSURE: Full sun.

PROPAGATION METHODS:

Seed: Easily propagated from seed, which is readily available from garden shops in Hawai'i and possibly from mail order catalogs that handle Oriental vegetables. Sow in full sun, cover the seed lightly with soil, and keep moist. Seedlings are prone to

Chrysanthemum coronarium

damping-off—death due to fungal diseases that thrive in high humidity and still air; good air circulation and full sunlight minimize this problem.

Cuttings: 4- to 6-inch tip cuttings can be propagated by removing the leaves from the lower half and inserting the stem into a perlite and peat medium. These cuttings require bright light and good air circulation; if they are kept in shade with too much moisture, the leaves tend to rot.

Division: Not applicable.

CULTURAL PRACTICES: Grown as a winter annual by local gardeners, who do not let the plants reach flowering size before harvesting. In full sun the plant is self-branching, developing into a bright green, attractive plant. Pinching shoot tips of immature plants promotes a fuller, symmetrical growth habit.

PESTS: Leaf miners and red spider mites can be problems in some gardens.

COMMENTS: Fast growing.

Citrus hystrix deCandolle

Rutaceae, the citrus family

COMMON NAMES: English: Kaffir lime, double leaf lime, leech lime; Thai: *ma krut.*

DESCRIPTION: Shrub or low tree 6 to 35 feet tall, many branched and spiny, the crown dense and twiggy, young stems angular and slightly compressed. Leaves alternate, petiole broadly winged, 0.25–3 inches long, the wings obovate to obcordate, sometimes running into the blade, blade oblong-ovate to orbicular-ovate, 1.25–6 inches × 1–2.5 inches, leathery, dark green, and glossy on the upper side, duller, paler green, and heavily dotted with pellucid glands below, aromatic when bruised. Inflorescences axillary or terminal, dense, 1–5-flowered. Flowers fragrant, shortly stalked, the calyx 4-lobed, yellowish white with violet margins, petals 4 or 5, ovate-oblong, up to 0.4 inch long, yellowish white or tinged with red, stamens 24–30, free, ovary flattened globose, glabrous, style short. Fruit pendulous, globose, wrinkled, and roughened (warty), yellow when ripe, the peel thick and yellowish green, inner pulp yellowish, very sour, and slightly bitter. Seeds ovoid-oblong.

DISTRIBUTION: The native range of this species is not known with certainty but it is widely cultivated throughout Indonesia, Malaysia, the Philippines, Myanmar, Southeast Asia, Sri Lanka, and parts of India. It is likely that the Kaffir lime originated somewhere in the Indo-Malayan region.

USE: In Thai and Laotian cooking, the fresh leaves are shredded or minced and added to soups, fish patties, curries, and other cooked dishes, where they add a distinctive flavor that is difficult to duplicate. In local markets the leaves are sold either fresh or dried; on the mainland only dried leaves are readily available, although the demand for fresh ones has prompted herb growers in Florida and California to begin growing this species. The fruit rind is used—mainly dried—as an ingredient in curry pastes, but the juice is never used. In many tropical Asian countries the fruit juice is used in shampooing the hair and is believed to kill head lice.

EXPOSURE: Full sun.

PROPAGATION METHODS:

Seed: Not commonly done, because seedlings are slow growing.

Cuttings: Tip and stem cuttings 4 to 6 inches long will root easily in a 50:50 peat-perlite medium, particularly with overhead misting. The root strike is slow.

Division: Not applicable.

Citrus hystrix

Grafting: The best method is by grafting Kaffir lime onto disease resistant tangerine rootstocks. Air layering also works well.

CULTURAL PRACTICES: Kaffir lime develops into a typical citrus tree with a dense crown of twiggy growth armed with sharp straight spines. It is recommended that dead internal branches be thinned out to facilitate air circulation and light penetration. The spines are hazardous when pruning. The Kaffir lime requires full sunlight from all sides for healthy growth. It adapts well to container growth and is handy to keep nearby for Asian cooking.

PESTS: The Kaffir lime is plagued by scale, mealy bugs, and aphids, which can be reduced with good air circulation between the branches. Since the leaves are eaten, pesticides cannot safely be used; pests can be mitigated by regular applications of soapy water solution (1 or 2 tablespoons of dish detergent per quart of water). Oil-based sprays (such as Volck oil spray) will kill scale and prevent the spread of sooty mold, which blackens the foliage. Virus infection turns the leaves yellow and will eventually kill the plant. African snails *(Achatina fulica)* will devour tender young foliage. Snails may be removed by hand at night while they are feeding, or apply a circle of agricultural lime around the tree just before dark. Alternatively, snail and slug pellets may be applied every two weeks if the problem persists.

COMMENTS: The growth rate is slow and roots develop faster in well-drained soils. Fertilizing three or four times per year with a balanced citrus food will alleviate this. Kaffir lime makes a fine container specimen, although the sharp spines are hazardous.

Coriandrum sativum Linnaeus
Apiaceae (or Umbelliferae), the parsley family

COMMON NAMES: English: Chinese parsley, coriander greens, cilantro; Chinese: *xiang cai, yuen sai;* Japanese: *koyendoro;* Lao: *hap kom, phak hom pom, phak houa pom;* Okinawan: *kushiba;* Pilipino: *kulantro;* Spanish: *culantro;* Thai: *phak chee;* Vietnamese: *cay ngo, ngo, rau mai, rau ngo tan.*

DESCRIPTION: Annual herbs 8–28 inches tall, all parts glabrous, arising from a thickened taproot. Basal leaves deeply 3-lobed, the leaflets fan shaped to ovate in outline, margins toothed or incised, the median and upper leaves becoming progressively more divided, the ultimate lobes threadlike and entire. Inflorescence a terminal compound umbel. Flowers small, petals white or faintly pinkish. Fruit round, smooth, about 0.2 inch in diameter, separating into 2 hemispherical mericarps, each containing a single seed.

DISTRIBUTION: Presumed to be native originally to the Mediterranean region and now found worldwide as both a cultivated herb and a weed. The species is unknown in the wild state.

USE: Almost all parts of the plant are useful. The root is scraped and pounded as an integral component of Thai curry pastes and marinades for grilled meats. The basal leaves and their petioles are "probably the most widely used of all flavoring herbs throughout the world" (Stuart 1979), and appear in salads, soups, curries, stews, cold marinades, pestos, and a vast assortment of dishes in cuisines from every part of the world. The dry ripe fruits ("seeds") are the spice coriander, used in baking, curry powders, making liqueurs, confectionery, and for potpourris. The upper (cauline or stem) leaves are not used because of their strong and unpleasant odor and flavor.

EXPOSURE: Full sun in winter; filtered sun in summer.

PROPAGATION METHODS:

Seed: Easily germinated from seed, although old seed can be slow to sprout. Soaking the seeds in hot water before planting will improve the germination rate. Sow seed in a sunny location where the seedlings can be shaded after they come up. Seeds are usually planted thick and then thinned out if they all come up. Coriander does not transplant well. If seedlings are to be transplanted, do so when they can be handled

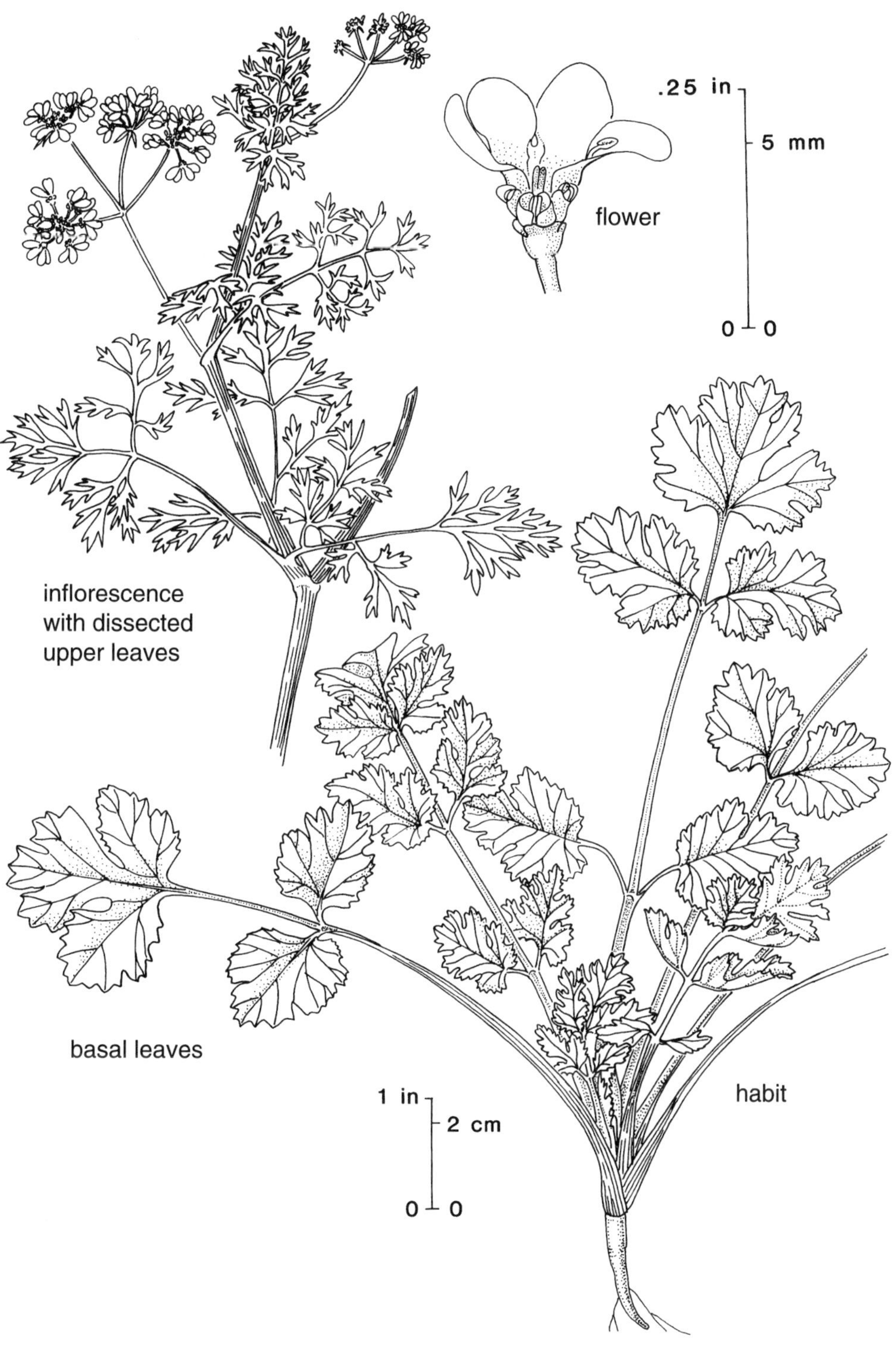

Coriandrum sativum

without damaging them, usually after the second true leaf develops. Leave them in the seeding container if the plant is to be used for its leaves.

Cuttings: Not applicable.

Division: Not applicable.

CULTURAL PRACTICES: This is a high-maintenance crop as an annual. Coriander is used both in the seedling and mature stages. Sometimes it tends to bolt prematurely in hot weather. The seed germinates well, and if seed is evenly dispersed the plants can be left to flower and produce seed. If the plant is grown for the seed, it can be transplanted as soon as it is handleable and planted 18 inches apart to mature. Coriander has a tap root and does not transplant successfully once the tap root has started developing. The immature plant is cultivated for cilantro and the young leaves are harvested before the plant matures. Harvest the mature seed and roots and discard the rest of the plant. Coriander grows best in well-drained, sandy soil.

PESTS: Insect pests have not been noticed. Zebra doves, so prevalent at low elevations in Hawai'i, will eat newly sown seed; netting or a wire-covered frame placed over the seed bed will exclude the birds until germination takes place.

COMMENTS: Very fast growing.

Cryptotaenia canadensis (Linnaeus) deCandolle

Synonym: *Cryptotaenia japonica* Hasskarl

Apiaceae (or Umbelliferae), the parsley family

COMMON NAMES: English: Japanese parsley in local usage, Japanese wild chervil, Japanese honewort; Chinese: *san ip, san ye qin, ya er qin;* Japanese: *mitsuba;* Okinawan: *mitsuba-zeri.*

DESCRIPTION: Glabrous perennial up to 2 feet tall with short rhizomes and rather thick roots. Lower leaves in a basal rosette, long petiolate, blade divided into 3 sessile leaflets, ovate to diamond-shaped in outline, the lateral ones asymmetrical at the base, the margins incised or shredded, rarely deeply lobed; stem leaves with petioles diminishing in length, uppermost ones sessile, blade becoming linear to lanceolate and often undivided. Inflorescence a tall, erect scape; umbellets 1–4-flowered, pedicels very unequal, flowers white. Fruit oblong-cylindrical, about 0.2 inch long.

DISTRIBUTION: *Cryptotaenia canadensis* is found throughout eastern North America, from New Brunswick south to Alabama and Georgia, and in eastern Asia, including China, Korea, and the Kurile Islands as well as the Japanese islands of Hokkaido, Honshu, Shikoku, Kyushu, and the Ryukyu Islands. Asian plants were formerly considered to be a distinct species, *C. japonica*, but Dr. Lincoln Constance, specialist in the Apiaceae, has advised us that plants from the two areas can scarcely be differentiated and he considers them all to belong to a single species. A plant of woods and hills, Japanese honewort forms a groundcover in shady places, flowering in June and July and fruiting in August. *Mitsuba* (meaning "three leaved") is frequently cultivated as a vegetable and herb in Japan. *Cryptotaenia canadensis* has escaped from cultivation in Hawai'i and is weedy in several places.

USE: The light green leaves are used fresh or blanched in soups and salads, lightly pickled in vinegar, and in fried foods. Both the petiole and blade are eaten. While easily grown from seed during the spring and summer months, the plants are also forced in special huts or frames during the rest of the year. The roots are fried and eaten.

EXPOSURE: Partial shade with protection from drying winds.

PROPAGATION METHODS:

Seed: Usually grown year-round from seed, which germinates readily. Since seed is not commercially available, it appears that local gardeners are saving and sharing it among themselves.

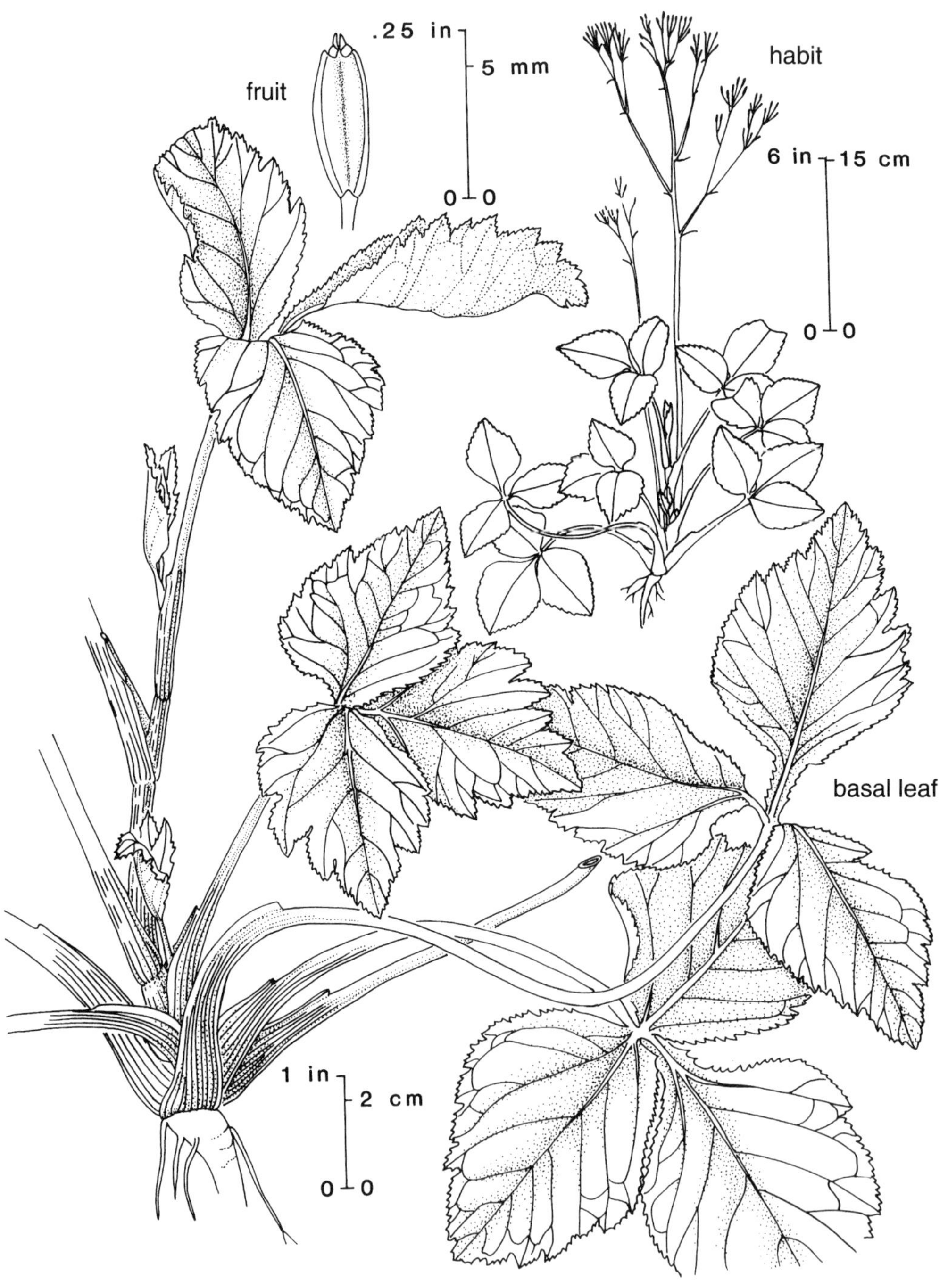

Cryptotaenia canadensis

Cuttings: Not used in Hawai'i. It was found upon experimenting that 5-inch tip cuttings rooted successfully in a 50:50 peat-perlite medium over bottom heat.

Division: When grown under ideal conditions, compound crowns will develop. These may be lifted with a spading fork, separating the crowns in the process. Each should be replanted into enriched soil and watered thoroughly.

CULTURAL PRACTICES: A prolific display of leaves develops from a single basal rosette. Plant 18 inches apart in filtered light. Removal of emerging flower spikes will stimulate continued production of leaves, the edible part of the plant. This is a low-maintenance plant unless it reseeds itself, in which case unwanted seedlings should be weeded out.

PESTS: Slugs can be a problem. An application of lime around plants will discourage and kill slugs. Do not, however, allow the lime to touch the leaves as they will turn black.

COMMENTS: Grows rapidly and can be weedy and invasive.

Curcuma longa Linnaeus

Zingiberaceae, the ginger family

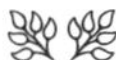

COMMON NAMES: English: turmeric, tumeric; Hawaiian: *'olena;* Japanese: *ukon;* Okinawan: *uccin;* Pilipino: *dilao, kulyao, kunig;* Thai: *khamin;* Vietnamese: *nghe, nghe kuong huynh.*

DESCRIPTION: Herb with leaf rosettes 1.5–4 feet tall, arising from an erect underground rhizome. Leaves 5–8, whorled, blade lanceolate, oblong, or elliptic, 12–28 inches × 3–10 inches, glabrous. Inflorescence terminal on the leafy shoot, half hidden among the leaves, cylindrical, 4–8 inches long and 2–3 inches in diameter, the bracts green, white, or pale pink. Flowers white, pale pink, yellowish, or greenish, the labellum broadly obovate, whitish or pale yellow with a yellow stripe down the center. Fruit not produced.

DISTRIBUTION: Probably native to India, but early on transported by man throughout tropical Asia and into the islands of the Pacific for its usefulness as a dye source, spice, and medicinal. This species is unknown in the wild, although it is cultivated throughout tropical Asia, Africa, Madagascar, the Pacific, and in many tropical American areas as well.

USE: The rhizome is the source of the culinary spice turmeric, an integral component of curry powders. The rhizomes also provide a deep yellow or orange dye and have been used in local medicine and cosmetics, as well as in religious observances, particularly among the Hindus.

EXPOSURE: Partial shade and protection from wind.

PROPAGATION METHODS:

Seed: This plant does not fruit and therefore does not produce seed. It is because this species is a sterile triploid (i.e., it has three sets of chromosomes instead of the usual two) that no fruits are produced.

Cuttings: The rhizomes, which are modified stems, are separated and cut into 4–6-inch lengths as cuttings. All root growth and soil particles are removed. Clean cuts are made through the rhizome before inserting for propagation.

Division: This plant is most easily grown by division. At the end of the growing season when the plant has become dormant (December), the rhizomes can be dug up with a spading fork and divided for replanting.

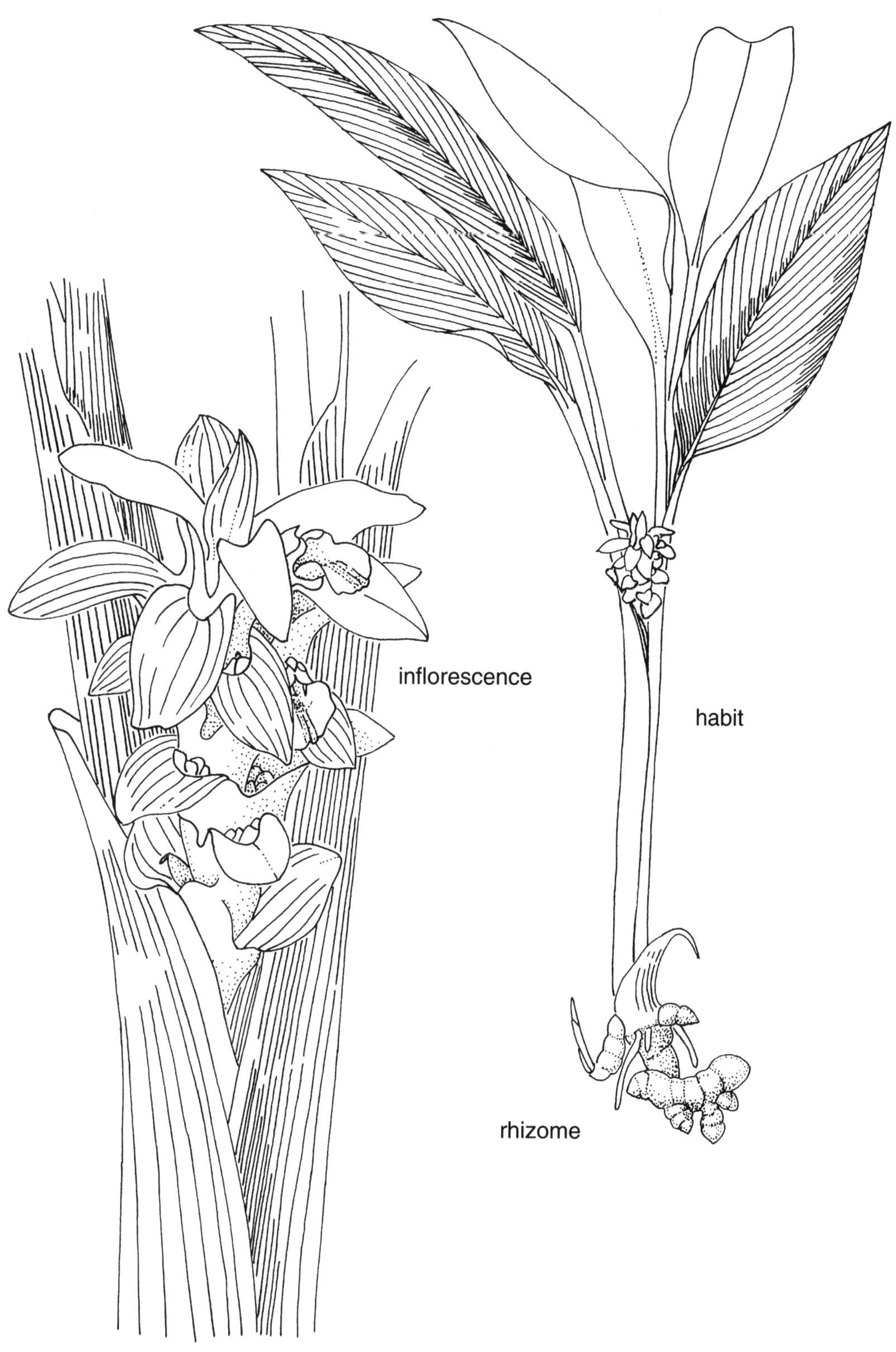

Curcuma longa

CULTURAL PRACTICES: When turmeric is in its dormant phase, division should occur. Immediately after planting, water once and do not water again until new growth emerges above ground. Water more frequently as the leaves develop. Plant 30–36 inches apart in well-drained organic loam, covering the rhizomes twice as deep as their diameter. If the plant is allowed to dry out, the leaf margins quickly turn brown.

PESTS: Borers will attack the rhizomes. To control this pest, lift affected plants with a spading fork, wash out the soil from the root mass, cut out any damaged portions, and dip thc hcalthy pieces in a malathion solution, diluted to standard spray application. Dry in a well-ventilated place. Replant as described above.

COMMENTS: Fast growing. Turmeric plants have a dormant period (winter/spring) when leaves die back and a growing season (summer/fall) when flowering and foliage development occur.

Cymbopogon citratus (Nees) Stapf

Poaceae (or Gramineae), the grass family

COMMON NAMES: English: lemon grass; Chinese: *xiang mao cao;* Pilipino: *barani, tanglad, salay, salaid;* Thai: *ta krai;* Vietnamese: *sa, xa.*

DESCRIPTION: Perennial, robust, clump-forming grass that grows in dense tufts 2–3 feet tall and about as large in diameter from short underground rhizomes. Leaves linear, narrow, drooping, the margins rough, pale green, the lower surface glaucous (having a waxy bloom like a plum). Inflorescence (rarely produced) a 4–6-foot-tall scape bearing a loose panicle of awnless, stalked spikelets.

DISTRIBUTION: Probably native to Sri Lanka, Malaysia, or Indonesia, but the exact provenance of lemon grass is unknown because it has been cultivated since antiquity and is unknown in the wild state. Today it is distributed throughout the tropics as a commercial and home garden crop, and it is also used as a soil binder to control erosion.

USE: In cooking, lemon grass leaves are used to flavor food and drinks throughout India, Southeast Asia, Malaysia, and Indonesia. The leaf blades are used, fresh or dried, to make a refreshing tea, and the tough, almost woody stalks composed of overlapping leaf bases are sliced and pounded as an ingredient in curry pastes, soups, stews, and many other foods. The solid stem parts are inserted into chicken cavities when roasting. Lemon grass is an integral ingredient for many tropical Asian cuisines, and is particularly associated with seafood dishes. It can be purchased sliced and dried or powdered in many ethnic markets, and in this form can be substituted in some—though by no means all—recipes.

Lemon grass is commercially valuable as the source of an essential oil that is widely used to scent soaps and shampoos as well as many kinds of technical preparations and for aldehydes that can be converted to other compounds, such as vitamin A. Commercial production of lemon grass for the essential oil occurs in Guatemala, Brazil, the West Indies, Congo, Tanzania, Madagascar, in Indochina, and on a small scale on the Wai‘anae Coast of O‘ahu. Lemon grass makes an excellent medicinal tea, reducing stuffiness and water retention. Apparently it is a diuretic and should not be excessively consumed.

CULTIVATION: Sandy soil, excellent drainage, and plenty of water are needed. Although fertile soils produce more luxuriant foliage, the oil content—and hence the flavor—is lower.

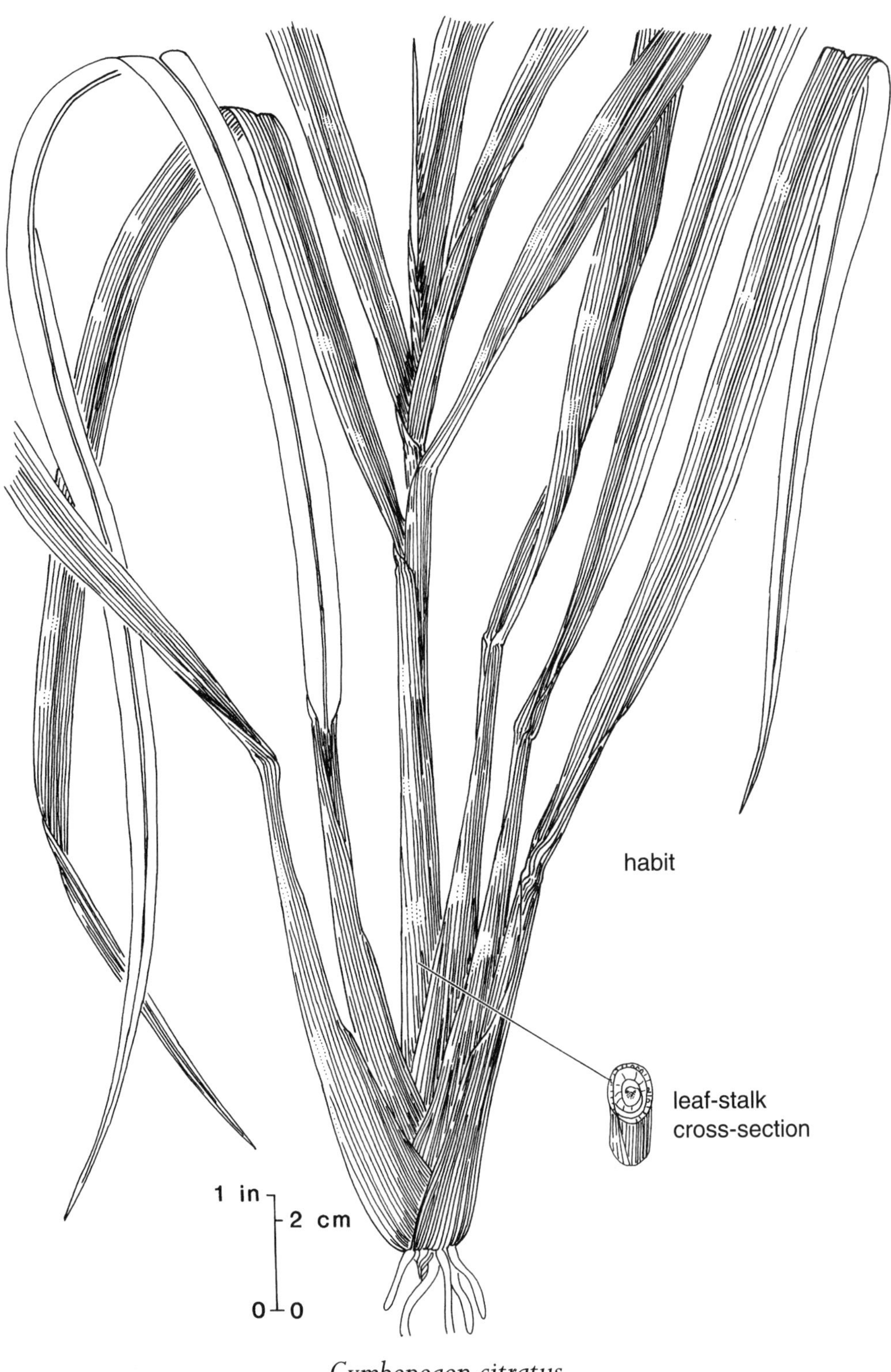

Cymbopogon citratus

EXPOSURE: Full sun is ideal. Partial shade results in spindly growth.

PROPAGATION METHODS:

Seed: Because inflorescences are rarely produced, lemon grass is not propagated by seed.

Cuttings: Lemon grass stalks are sold in 12- to 18-inch lengths, with the blades of the leaves trimmed off. Single stalks strike root readily when inserted in damp sand or stood upright with just the very base in shallow water, as long as the dormant buds in the basal rhizome have not been removed. Once rooted the stalks can be planted, taking care not to break the water roots. Keep these moist for a week after planting. After that the plant develops rapidly into a mature, grassy clump.

Division: Most frequently grown by division because the plant develops into robust clumps. When a large clump has developed, about 12 inches in diameter, dig up the entire clump and divide with a spading fork so as not to sever the roots. Cut the top of the plant to within 6–8 inches from the root and replant the divisions, each comprising three or four stalks. Water thoroughly. Between December and February is the best period for dividing clumps, although in Hawai'i this is often done at any time of the year.

CULTURAL PRACTICES: This can be an attractive garden plant when grown in masses for ornamental purposes. Usually one clump is adequate to supply the kitchen needs of one household. Numerous cultivars, differing in flavor and aroma, are available and some are more desirable than others. Plant 36 inches apart, or, for an instant specimen, plant divisions 8 inches apart in a clump. Water thoroughly, then reduce watering until vigorous new growth develops. Lemon grass thrives best in sandy, well-drained soils. Leaves sometimes may look scraggly. Trim the blades right into the center of the plant so new foliage will emerge. The red- or pink-colored leaf tips may sometimes turn brown from drying out. Lemon grass is an easily grown plant requiring very little maintenance.

PESTS: During the rainy season, a rust fungus *(Puccinia nakanishikii)* is prevalent on the foliage, leading to rejection of commercial export shipments of lemon grass. The orange-colored fungal bodies are found in the crown of the plant, where the leaf blades converge. Affected leaves should be cut off and destroyed (burned) or placed in the trash. Do not put in compost heap.

COMMENTS: Fast growing. Newly planted lemon grass appears slow growing until it is established; then the growth rate is rapid.

Elettaria cardamomum (Linnaeus) Maton
Zingiberaceae, the ginger family

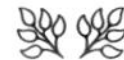

COMMON NAMES: English: cardamom, sometimes spelled "cardamon"; Thai: *krawaan thet.*

DESCRIPTION: A clump-forming, robust herbaceous plant, 6–15 feet tall. Rhizome woody, horizontal, stout, branched; roots in surface layers. Stems 10–20, erect, in a dense clump. Leaves in two ranks, petiole short, blade lanceolate, 10–36 inches × 2–6 inches, dark green above, sometimes hairy on the underside. Inflorescence arising from the rhizome at the base of the leafy stems, a panicle 2–4 feet long, prostrate, ascending or erect. Flowers orchidlike, about 1.5 inches long; petals pale green, the lip obovate, white with violet streaks radiating from the center. Fruit a 3-celled capsule, globose to ellipsoidal, pale green to yellow. Seeds 15–20 per fruit, dark brown, angled, rough coated, aromatic.

DISTRIBUTION: Cardamom is native in the western part of India between 2,100 and 5,000 feet elevation and also in Sri Lanka at similar altitudes. The wild plants grow in evergreen forests that have an open canopy, admitting light to the ground, and along stream banks. The species is cultivated on a commercial scale in the southern Indian states of Kerala, Mysorc, and Madras, in Sri Lanka, and in Guatemala.

USE: The whole dried fruit and the seeds removed from the shell are an important spice and flavoring material, said to be "the third most costly spice in the world" (Rosengarten 1973). Coffee is flavored with cardamom throughout the Arab world, and bread and pastry in Scandinavia depend upon it for the distinctive flavor it lends. The United States and other countries are minor consumers of cardamom, but it—or its essential oil—is integral to the flavoring of products as diverse as good curry powder, hamburger and sausage seasoning, perfumes, tobacco products, and some drugs.

EXPOSURE: Partial shade and a location protected from strong winds; the plant tends to look shabby when the leaves are shredded by excessive wind.

PROPAGATION METHODS:

Seed: Seeds are used in commercial plantings, but rarely by small-scale growers. Germination is erratic and some seeds may take months or years. Also, the seed is the useful part of this ginger, so it is rarely used for propagation.

Cuttings: Not applicable.

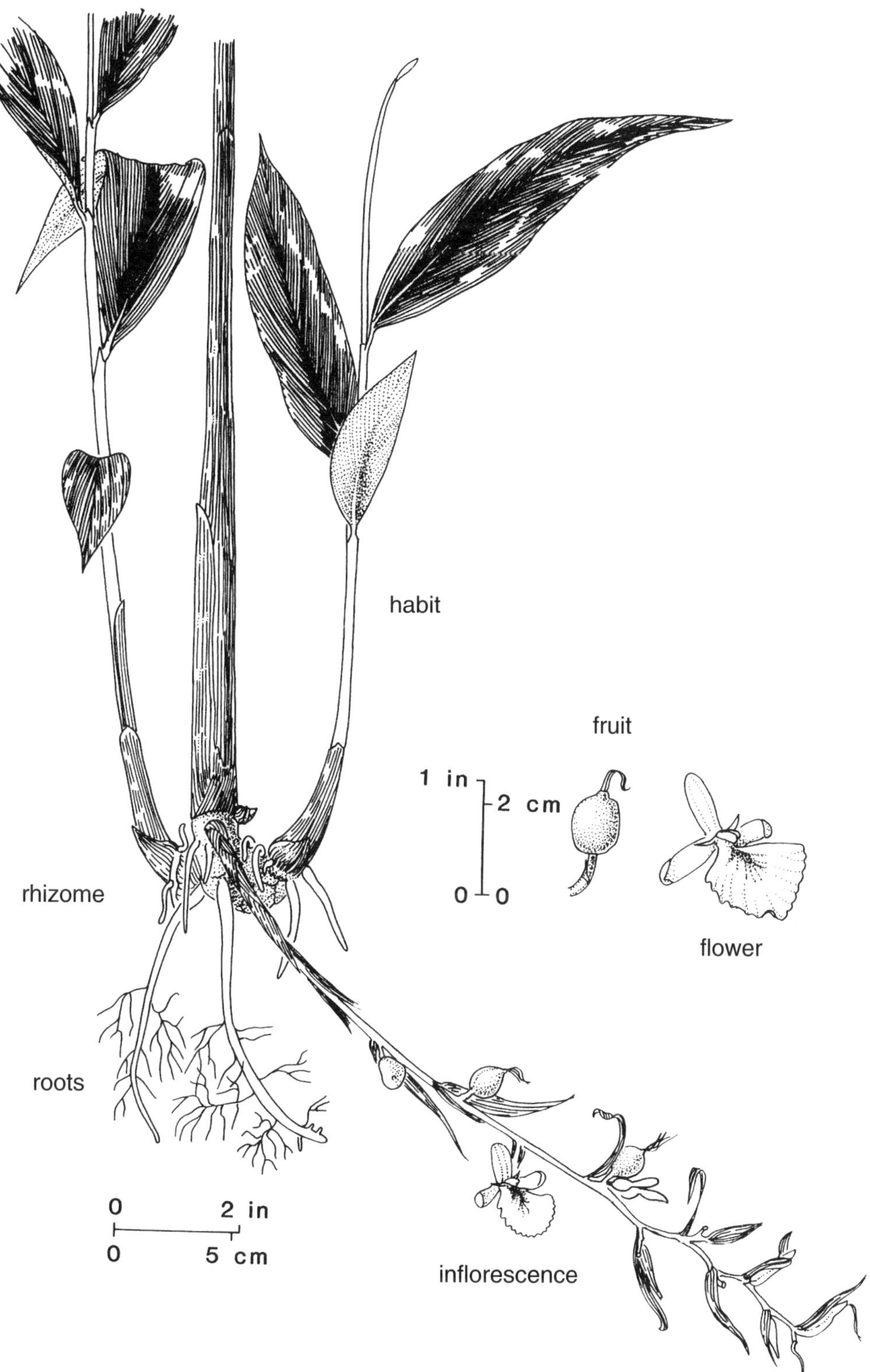

Elettaria cardamomum

Division: Woody rhizomes are divided during the dormant season (December through February in Hawai'i).

CULTURAL PRACTICES: The woody rhizomes are divided into 6-inch lengths and planted 3 inches deep and 36 inches apart. A well-drained, organically fertile soil is recommended, although cardamom also grows in heavy clay soils. Dense clumps develop that are useful as background plants. After flowering, the stems are cut to ground level, from where new canes emerge. Clumps should be divided and replanted once the surface area is filled with rhizomes or when growth deteriorates, especially noticeable when stems reach no more than 3 feet in height. Because the inflorescence is often prostrate, arising from the base of the stem, the seeds are difficult to harvest unless adequate space is provided around the plants.

PESTS: No pests have been observed.

COMMENTS: Relatively slow growing. When grown from seed, a cardamom plant may take four or five years before it flowers and bears fruit.

Allium tuberosum (garlic chive)

Alpinia galanga (galanga)

Artemisia vulgaris (mugwort)

Artemisia vulgaris (mugwort)

Boesenbergia rotunda (Chinese key)

Boesenbergia rotunda (Chinese key)

Capsicum annuum (chili pepper)

Capsicum annuum (chili pepper)

Capsicum baccatum (chili pepper)

Capsicum baccatum (chili pepper)

Left and above: Chrysanthemum coronarium (garland chrysanthemum)

Left and above: Citrus hystrix (Kaffir lime)

Coriandrum sativum
(Chinese parsley, coriander greens)

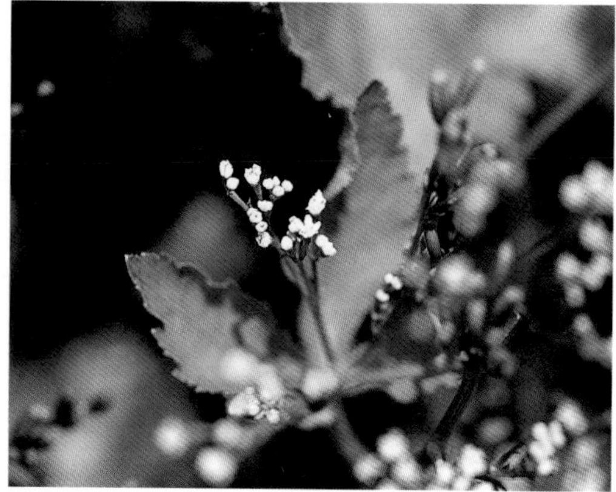

Cryptotaenia canadensis (Japanese parsley)

Curcuma longa (turmeric)

Cymbopogon citratus
(lemon grass)

Left and above: Elettaria cardamomum (cardamom)

Eryngium foetidum (thorny coriander)

Hemerocallis (daylily)

Houttuynia cordata (houttuynia)

Limnophila chinensis subsp. *aromatica* (rice-paddy herb)

Eryngium foetidum Linnaeus

Apiaceae (or Umbelliferae), the parsley family

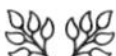

COMMON NAMES: English: thorny coriander, saw-leaf herb; Chinese: *jia yuan qian;* Lao: *hom tay;* Spanish: *culantro;* Thai: *pak chi farang;* Vietnamese: *cay muoy than, cay nuitau, cay ngo tan, ngo gai, ngo ta.*

DESCRIPTION: Annual or biennial plant arising from a thickened rootstock, with a basal rosette of 6–20 oblanceolate to oblong leaves, the blade running onto the petiole, the margins spiny or finely toothed, the apex rounded to blunt. Flowers borne in a dense cylindrical head about 1 inch long on an erect stalk 4–12 inches tall, the head subtended by 5–7 leafy bracts, these spiny margined and eventually reflexed downward; the individual flowers are minute, petals pale bluish or greenish white. Seed very tiny, dark brown.

DISTRIBUTION: Native in the New World tropics from southern Mexico to Panama and in the West Indies; now weedy and cultivated in tropical regions of Asia and Africa. It is grown on Oʻahu for export to West Coast Asian markets and restaurants.

USE: Grown in Southeast Asia as a culinary herb, as it is on several islands of the West Indies. The leaves have a strong-smelling odor because they contain aldehyde compounds. *Ngo gai* is served raw with the Vietnamese beef noodle soup *(pho)* and is used similarly to coriander *(Coriandrum sativum)* in other Vietnamese dishes. The plant has medicinal uses throughout tropical Asia.

EXPOSURE: Full sun.

PROPAGATION METHODS:

Seed: The fine seed self-sows very easily. To germinate the seed, mix it with a finely screened tablespoon of dry peat moss. Distribute the seed/peat mixture over a seed bed with a sandy, well-drained medium. Water with a very fine sprinkling head or mist with a spray bottle. Transplant seedlings when they are large enough to handle.

Cuttings: Not applicable.

Division: Crown divisions are used locally, but success rates are poor.

CULTURAL PRACTICES: Plant out in sandy soil 18 inches apart. To encourage tender young shoots, pinch tips continuously and prevent flowering to encourage basal growth. This biennial is short lived in tropical climates.

PESTS: Leaf miners occasionally trouble this herb.

COMMENTS: Very fast growing.

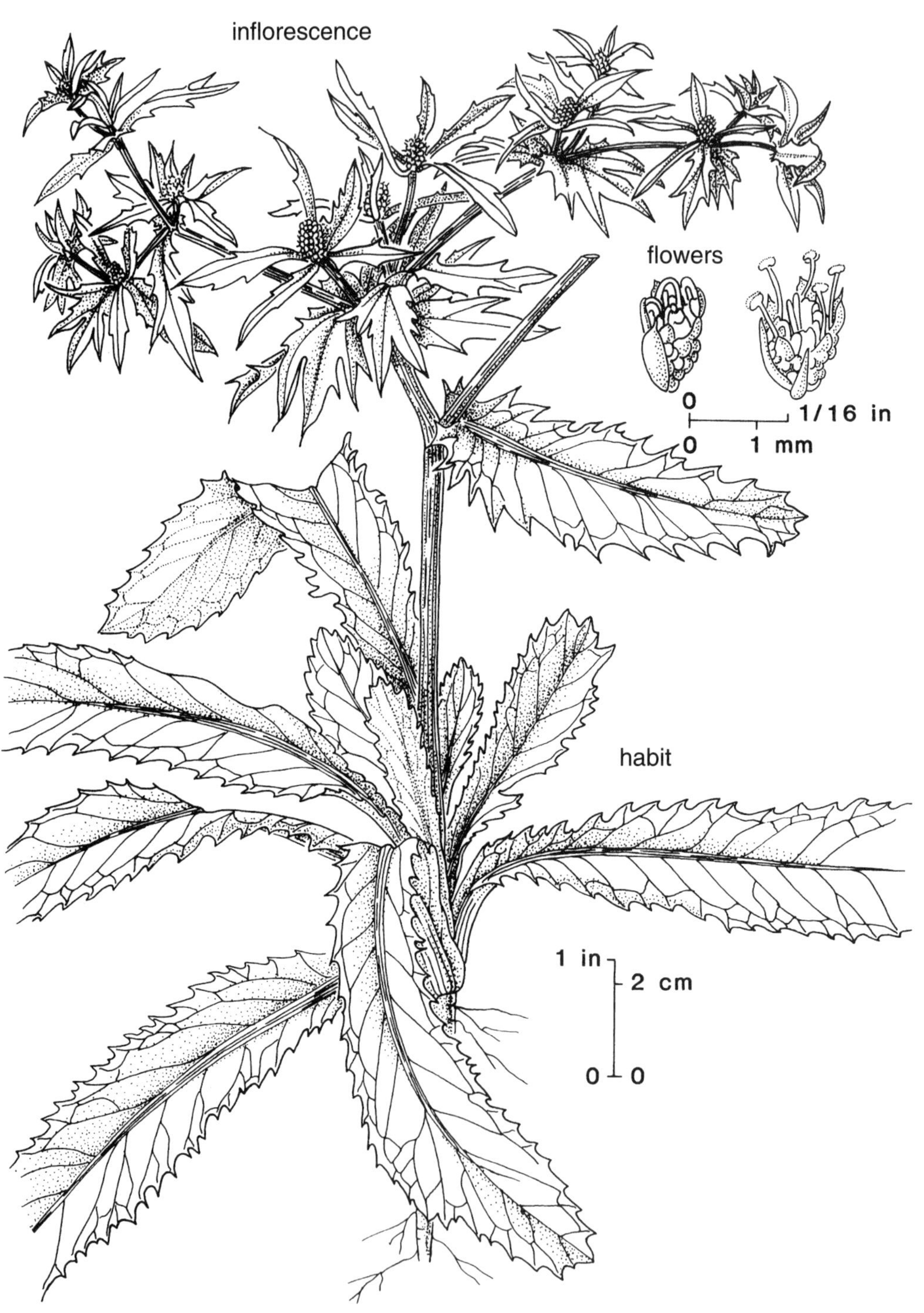

Eryngium foetidum

Hemerocallis species and hybrids
Liliaceae (sometimes Amaryllidaceae), the lily family

COMMON NAMES: English: daylily; Chinese: *jin-pi, gum-chum, kim-choi;* Japanese: *kanzō, karizo, wasuregusa;* Okinawan: *kanso;* Thai: *dok mai cheen, dok mai jin.*

DESCRIPTION: Herbaceous clump-forming perennial from an underground rhizome; roots fleshy and swollen, especially near their tips. Leaves distichous (in 2 opposite ranks or rows), deciduous or evergreen, blades linear, flat or folded toward the base, recurved. Inflorescence a raceme or panicle atop a solid stalk; bracts small or large and leaflike. Flowers last a single day; corolla broadly funnel shaped, petals fused into a tube at base, free above, broadly ovate, yellow or orange, sometimes reddish; stamens 6, attached at mouth of corolla tube, deflexed; ovary inferior, 3-celled; style threadlike. Fruit a dehiscent capsule, often 3-angled or 3-winged.

DISTRIBUTION: The fifteen species of the genus *Hemerocallis* are distributed through eastern Asia in Manchuria, China, Korea, and Japan. Various species have been cultivated in that region for centuries and many of the plants grown in gardens today are of hybrid origin. Daylilies are now grown the world over as ornamentals.

USE: Several species of *Hemerocallis* provide edible parts that are used in various countries. The young leaves are eaten as a vegetable by the Japanese. The mature flower buds are dried as a flavoring and vegetable in China, and the fresh buds are eaten in China and North America as a vegetable and in salads. The delicate flavor is reminiscent of asparagus and combines well with chicken. When used in stronger-flavored dishes, such as hot and sour soup, the buds provide texture and bulk rather than flavor. Dried buds are soaked in hot water for fifteen to thirty minutes, and after the hard ovary is cut off the whole buds can be knotted (so they don't disintegrate during cooking) or shredded. Fresh buds can be washed and the stamens and pistil removed before the petals are eaten.

EXPOSURE: Full sun in sheltered areas or light shade in very hot, dry situations. The soil should not be allowed to dry out if plants are in an exposed situation.

PROPAGATION METHODS:

Seed: Propagated from seed by professional growers. Rarely used by the home gardener.

Cuttings: Not propagated by cuttings, but can be by viviparous plantlets. These plantlets are found on the flower scape and can be broken off and inserted into a growth medium. These tend to grow fairly rapidly.

Division: This is the most common form of propagation because of the rapid

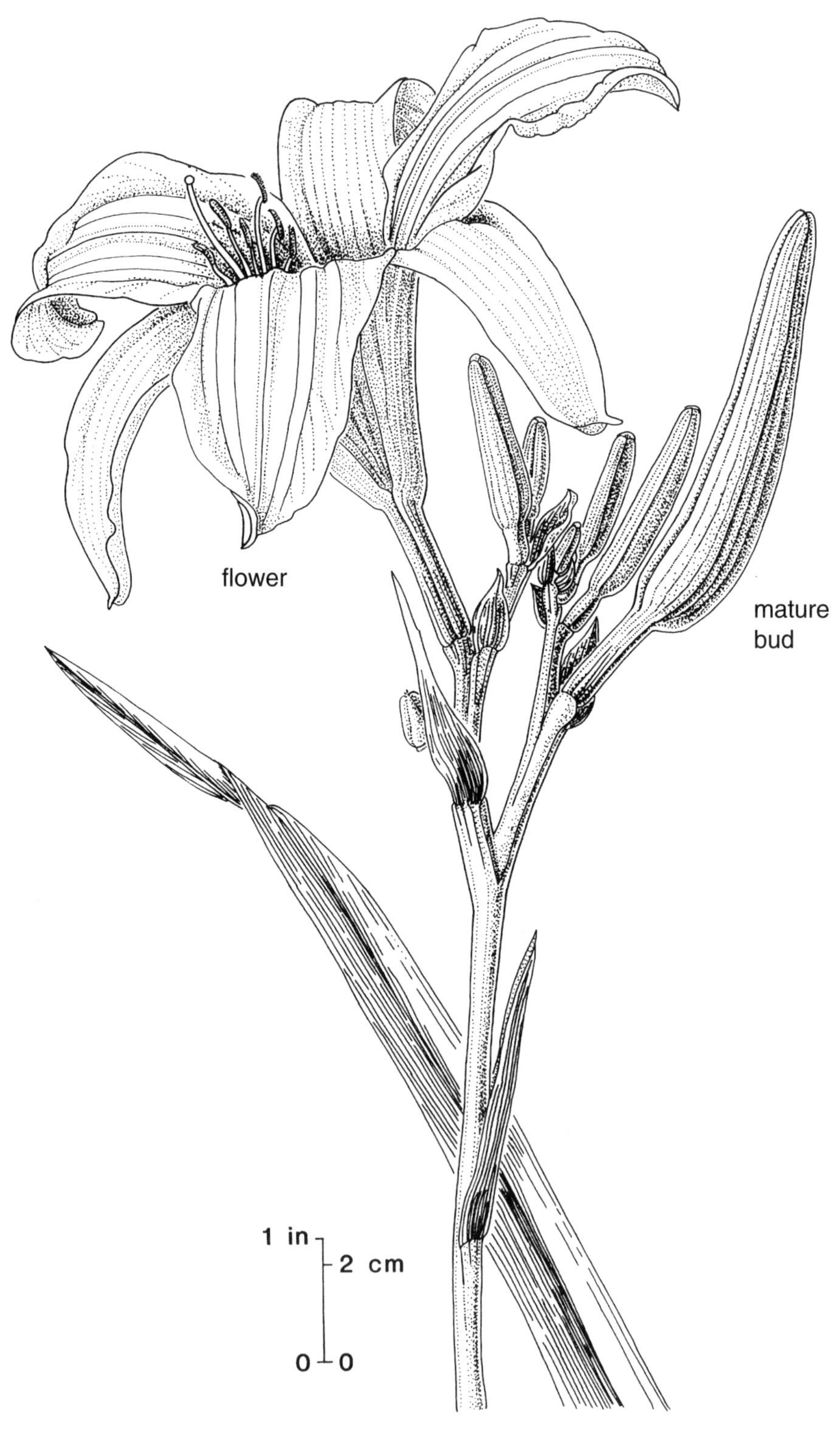

Hemerocallis

increase of the root crown. Using a spading fork, insert into the root crown and ease the clump apart. Individual plants can be separated for planting. Either leave the top growth or cut the tops off completely for faster regeneration of the leaf growth. Sometimes the roots will be a heavy mass of tangled, thickened storage roots that can be severed without impact to the plant.

CULTURAL PRACTICES: *Hemerocallis* species come in three size classes: small, medium, and large. Some are evergreen and others deciduous. They flower either seasonally or sporadically. If planted in pots, the daylily is slow in developing leafy growth, but the roots enlarge and quickly fill the container. When planted in the ground, spacing should be 12–18 inches apart, depending upon the size of the mature plants. The soil should be enriched with one-third organic matter spaded to a depth of 9–10 inches, and a 2-inch-thick mulch between plants enhances growth. *Hemerocallis* should not be heavily fertilized as this produces excessive foliage. The maintenance required is minimal and consists of removing the old flower spikes and yellowing leaves for evergreen types.

PESTS: None observed.

COMMENTS: Fast growing. Daylilies are better known as ornamentals than as herbs. They are fine ground cover and foundation plants and are often used as an accompaniment in garden composition.

Houttuynia cordata Thunberg

Saururaceae, the lizard's tail family

COMMON NAMES: English: *houttuynia;* Chinese: *chu tsai, yu xing cao;* Japanese: *dokudami;* Thai: *phak khao thong, phluu kae;* Vietnamese: *giap ca, rau giap ca.*

DESCRIPTION: Perennial, deciduous, herbaceous plants, proliferating by slender horizontal stolons that give rise to thin, erect stems from 6 inches to 2 feet tall. Leaves alternate, simple, blade heart shaped, about 3 inches long and nearly as wide. Flowers minute and condensed into an oblong, erect head, the whole inflorescence subtended by 4 white, petal-like bracts and resembling a miniature dogwood *(Cornus).* Fruit a tiny obovoid capsule containing many seeds.

DISTRIBUTION: Native from the Himalayas in Nepal through eastern Asia to Japan and Taiwan; also in cooler mountainous areas of the tropics as far south as Java.

USE: Fresh leaves are used as a garnish for fish stew, fertilized duck eggs, and in salads. Two "flavors" are recognized: the Japanese type *(dokudami)* is scented of oranges; the Chinese type *(chu tsai, yu xing cao)* smells like raw meat, fish, or coriander leaves. Both chemotypes are used as food by the Vietnamese. The plant has minor medicinal uses in China. Thais eat raw leaves with *nam phrik* or *laab.*

There is a variegated form of *houttuynia,* the leaves streaked with red and white, that is grown as an ornamental. The typical form makes an effective ground cover for a shady, moist spot.

CULTIVATION: Plants are hardy at least to Zone 5, although the plants die down to ground level at the first frost. Propagation is usually by stem cuttings, which root easily.

EXPOSURE: In Hawai'i, partial sun to full shade seems to produce the best results, although in temperate climates *houttuynia* can be grown in full sun.

PROPAGATION METHODS:

Seed: Not usually grown from seed locally.

Cuttings: Stem tip cuttings 4–6 inches in length inserted in a 50:50 perlite-peat medium. Keep well watered and remove all flower buds during root development.

Division: Stolons develop rapidly and root approximately every inch at nodal joints. Stolons can be forked away from the plant crown and separated into 4–6-inch lengths and replanted 8–10 inches apart. When transplanting and replanting, prune

Houttuynia cordata

the aerial stems to a height of 4 inches before replanting. Water thoroughly after transplanting.

CULTURAL PRACTICES: Plants develop rapidly, sending stolons in all directions, becoming a loose, attractive woodland groundcover. A rich organic humus is recommended. To encourage a denser plant mass, pinching of shoot tips is recommended initially. This species does best when replanted yearly.

The plants will spread horizontally from the point where they are planted and are potentially invasive. It is best to plant them in a confined space or container. Drier conditions also inhibit vigorous growth and will keep them within bounds.

PESTS: Mealy bugs tend to develop on the stolons underground. Infested plants may be dug up, the roots and stolons flushed with a strong stream of water, and the cleaned pieces replanted. Several applications of soap and water will inhibit the spread of mealy bugs in the ground.

COMMENTS: Fast growing.

Limnophila chinensis (Osbeck) Merrill subsp. ***aromatica*** (Lamarck) Yamazaki

Synonym: *Limnophila aromatica* (Lamarck) Merrill

Scrophulariaceae, the snapdragon family

COMMON NAMES: English: rice-paddy herb, *ambulia;* Chinese: *shui fu rong;* Japanese: *shiso kusa;* Thai: *phak khayaeng;* Vietnamese: *rau ngo, rau om, ngo om.*

DESCRIPTION: Aquatic perennial, aromatic when bruised; stems sprawling, upturned at tips, firm-fleshy, glabrous or finely glandular. Leaves opposite or in whorls of three, sessile, blade lanceolate to ovate-lanceolate, 0.5–2.25 inches × 0.13–0.66 inch, punctate, entirely glabrous, margins finely toothed, base partially surrounding the stem, the apex acute. Flowers rarely produced in cultivation, borne singly in axils of upper leaves, pedicels up to 0.75 inch long, bracteoles 2, corolla trumpet shaped, white to pale or dark blue, or purple, the tube paler and woolly inside. Fruit (also rarely produced in cultivation) a compressed capsule about 0.25 inch long, brown, capped by the persistent style.

DISTRIBUTION: This subspecies of the widespread and variable *L. chinensis* is found in India, Sri Lanka, Southeast Asia, China, southern and central Japan, Malaysia, Indonesia, New Guinea, and northern Australia where it grows in wet prairies, rice paddies, pools and ponds near human habitations, and a variety of other damp or wet situations. It is apparently a recent introduction to Hawai'i, probably having been brought here by Vietnamese and Laotian immigrants.

USE: Rice-paddy herb is a common plant throughout its natural range and is used in a variety of culinary preparations. The Vietnamese eat the fresh leaves and use them in sweet and sour dishes and in soups. The leaves and stem tips are finely chopped and served in sour seafood soup, often with peeled, sliced taro leafstalks.

EXPOSURE: Full sun.

PROPAGATION METHODS:

Seed: Rarely produces flowers; therefore not propagated by seed.

Cuttings: Rice-paddy herb is easily propagated by stem cuttings rooted in water or planted directly into saturated soil. We found that 3–4-inch-long stem cuttings worked well in rooting medium. Make a cut below the node and remove all the lower sets of leaves, then insert in a 50:50 peat-perlite medium over bottom heat. Strong roots formed in fourteen days with bottom heat and twenty-one days without, although in the latter case rooting was erratic. Keep moist and shaded until rooted.

Division: Not applicable.

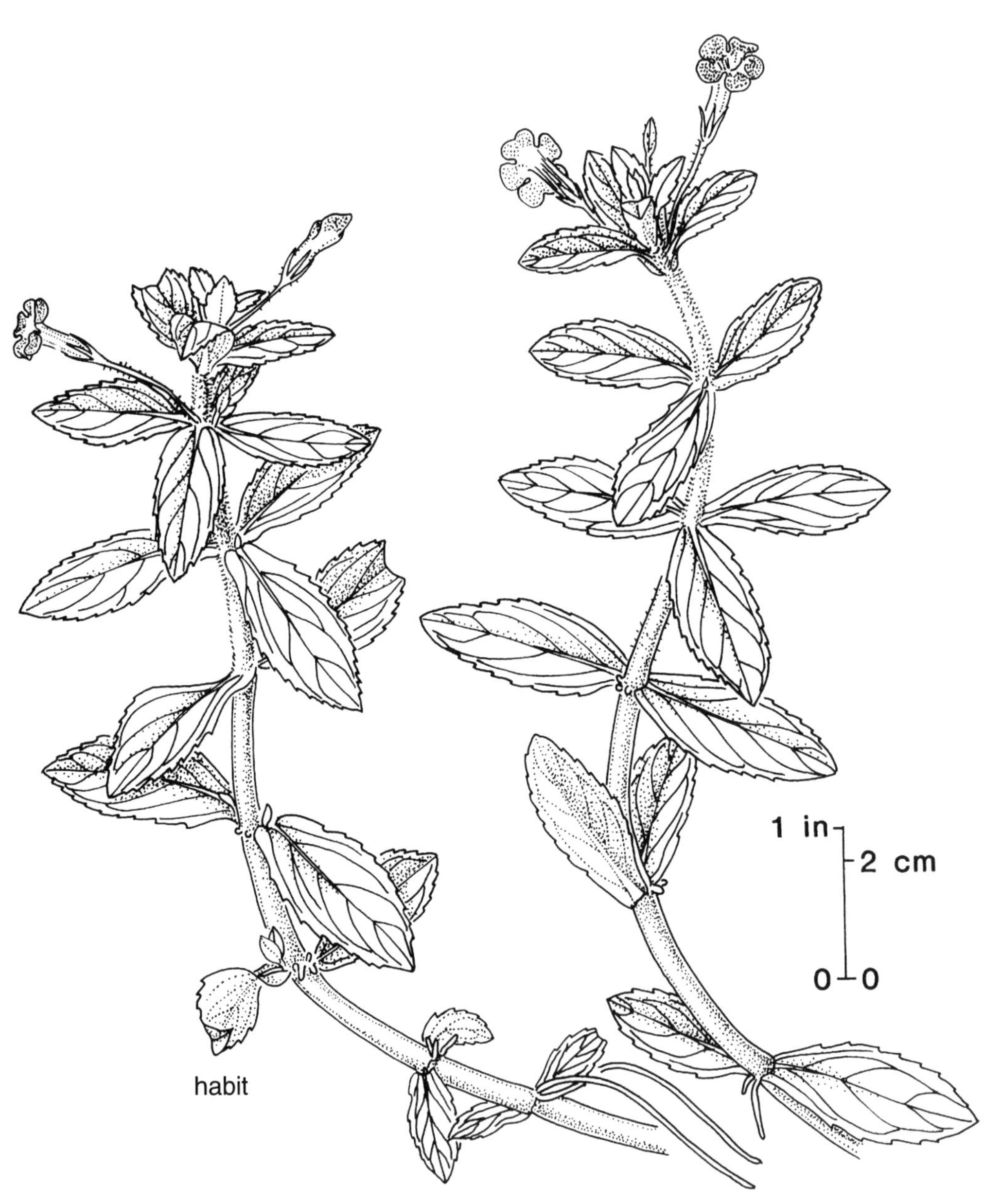

Limnophila chinensis subsp. *aromatica*

CULTURAL PRACTICES: Plant 6 inches apart in a clay soil in a shallow aquatic planting area. Pinch regularly to encourage dense branching. This plant is best started each year by discarding the old perennial plant and starting new cuttings. *Limnophila* will grow in a container in a heavy, moisture-retaining medium. Rapid growth tends to produce a scraggly appearance; pruning to a 3–4-inch length encourages side branching and a fuller appearance.

PESTS: No pests have been identified.

COMMENTS: Ideal for shallow water gardens or for a submerged pot in the margin of a deeper pond. Very fast growth rate.

Lippia micromera Schauer

Verbenaceae, the verbena family

COMMON NAMES: English: In Hawai'i, Mexican oregano, Spanish thyme; Spanish: *oregano del pais, oregano poleo.*

DESCRIPTION: A straggling, strongly aromatic shrub up to 7 feet tall, usually smaller, many branched, the branches downy and angular. Leaves opposite, crowded at nodes, shortly petiolate, the blade obovate to elliptic, 0.25–0.33 inch long, strongly creased above along the midrib and main veins, the margins slightly to strongly recurved, downy hairy on both sides, the underside also with resinous dots. Inflorescence a hemispherical head borne on a short stalk in the axil of the upper leaves; flowers tiny, sweetly fragrant, tubular with a flaring limb, white with a yellow throat.

DISTRIBUTION: Native presumably to northern South America (Colombia, Venezuela, Guyana), the Caribbean (Cuba, Hispaniola, Puerto Rico), and to Nicaragua. The plant has been widely distributed through cultivation and occurs in many other places as well.

USE: The fresh leaves are used as seasoning for meat, soup, gravy, and stuffing, and the plants are cultivated in kitchen gardens for this purpose. In some areas, small bundles of the twigs with leaves attached are sold in markets as herbs. The leaves are also used in local folk medicines.

EXPOSURE: Full sun.

PROPAGATION METHODS:

Seed: Rarely propagated by seed.

Cuttings: Grown by 4–6-inch tip and stem cuttings. Make a clean, sharp cut below the node and remove all the lower sets of leaves. The tip cuttings should be partly woody for a good strike. Tip cuttings that are too soft tend to dehydrate and either take much longer to strike, or die. The fully woody stem cuttings take longer to strike than the tips. These will root with #1 hormone in a very bright light.

Division: Not applicable.

CULTURAL PRACTICES: Plant in a full sun exposure in a sandy, well-drained loam. *Lippia* reaches 7 feet in height but can be pruned much smaller. Growths tend to emerge in all directions. These long growths can be left and the internal, crossover growths removed as they develop. *Lippia* develops strong, healthy growth in bright sun.

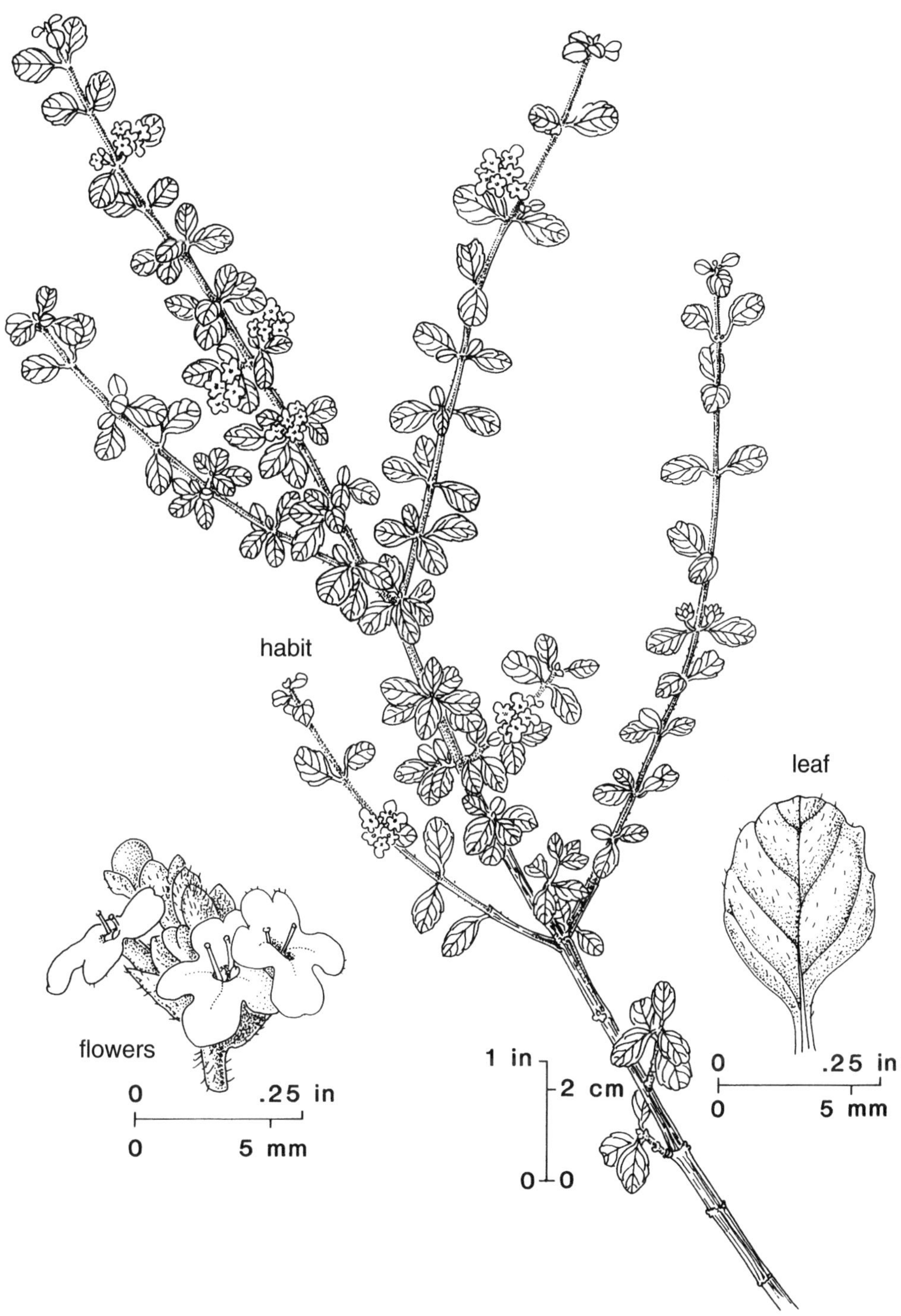

Lippia micromera

PESTS: None have been observed.

COMMENTS: The plant is moderate in growth rate. This can be an attractive plant if treated as a shrub with at least 4–5 feet in which to grow; it could make a fine bonsai or dwarf plant. The white flowers that are borne along the stems are attractive, especially if the plant is cultivated correctly.

Lippia origanoides Kunth

Verbenaceae, the verbena family

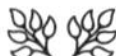

COMMON NAMES: English: In Hawai'i, Mexican oregano; Spanish: *oregano de burro, culantro cimarron.*

DESCRIPTION: A compact shrub 3–6 feet tall, many branched, and with 3-angled stems. Leaves opposite, parchment-textured and rough, blade elliptic-ovate, margins finely toothed, apex pointed, the upper side grayish green, the lower side paler. Inflorescences are axillary, often paired, and comprise a compact ellipsoidal head with overlapping bracts. Flowers are sweetly fragrant, the corollas white with a yellow throat, or purple. Seeds minute.

DISTRIBUTION: Native to dry rocky areas of Colombia, Venezuela, and south to Brazil (Morton 1981).

USE: The fresh leaves are used as a seasoning for sauces, especially for pork. In Hawai'i the leaves are used as a substitute for oregano and are shipped to the mainland fresh for sale on the West Coast. The leafy branch tips are sold in the markets of Venezuela, where they are used to prepare various medicinals.

EXPOSURE: Full sun.

PROPAGATION METHODS:

Seed: Not commonly propagated by seed. The fine seed can be mixed with 1 tablespoon of clean river sand or dry peat moss and dispersed over the surface of the seed bed, then covered very lightly with damp peat moss and watered with a fine spray from a sprinkling head.

Cuttings: Most often grown by 4–6-inch tip and stem cuttings. Make a clean, sharp cut below the node and remove all the lower sets of leaves. The tip cuttings should have a springy, crisp texture for a good strike. Some tip cuttings may be too soft and will tend to dehydrate and not strike. The woody stem cuttings take longer to strike than the tips. These will root with #1 hormone in a very bright light.

Division: Not applicable.

CULTURAL PRACTICES: Plant in a full sun exposure at least 6 feet apart in a sandy, well-drained loam. *Lippia* grows to 6 feet in height but can be pruned smaller. Growths tend to emerge in all directions. These long growths can be left and the internal, crossover growths removed as they develop. This can be an attractive plant if treated as a shrub with at least 4–6 feet in which to grow. The white flowers that are borne along the stems are attractive, especially if the plant is cultivated correctly.

PESTS: No pests observed.

COMMENTS: Moderate growth rate.

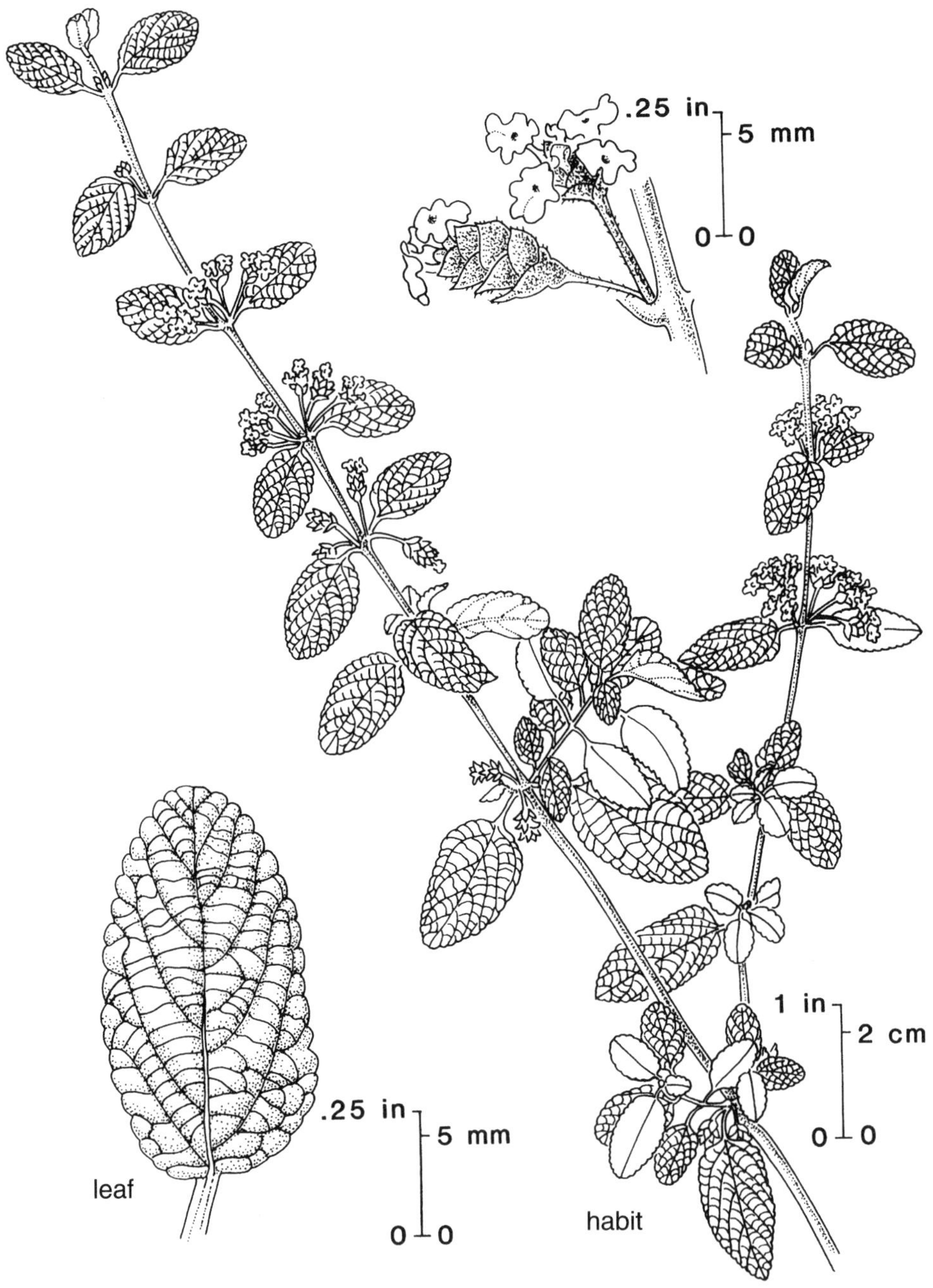

Lippia origanoides

Lippia micromera (Mexican oregano)

Lippia origanoides (Mexican oregano)

Mentha aquatica (mint)

Moringa oleifera (horseradish tree)

Murraya koenigii (curry leaf tree)

Ocimum tenuiflorum (holy basil)

Left and above: Ocimum basilicum (sweet basil)

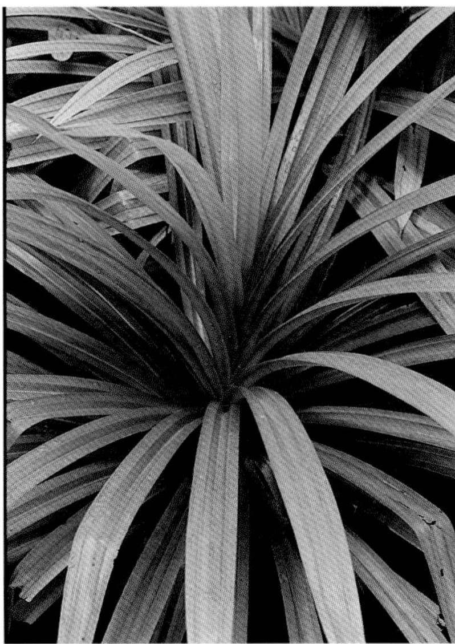

Pandanus amaryllifolius
(dwarf screw pine)

Peperomia pellucida (peperomia)

Perilla frutescens (beefsteak plant)

Piper lolot (lolot)

Above and right: Plectranthus amboinicus
(Greek oregano, Spanish thyme)

Polygonum odoratum (fragrant knotweed)

Polygonum odoratum (fragrant knotweed)

Solanum torvum (nightshade, turkeyberry)

Solanum torvum (nightshade, turkeyberry)

Tamarindus indica (tamarind)

Tamarindus indica (tamarind)

Zanthoxylum beechianum
(prickly ash, Okinawan sanshō)

Zingiber mioga (ginger bracts, *mioga* ginger)

Zingiber mioga (ginger bracts, *mioga* ginger)

Zingiber officinale (ginger, ginger root)

Mentha aquatica Linnaeus

Lamiaceae (or Labiatae), the mint family

COMMON NAMES: English: water mint, garden mint; Vietnamese: *hung dui, hung lang, lung que, rau hung, rau thom.*

DESCRIPTION: A sprawling perennial herb with creeping stems that spread horizontally beneath the soil, sending up erect, red-purple, squarish stems 12–18 inches tall. The leaves are sessile or very shortly petiolate, opposite, the blades oblong-elliptic, up to 2 inches long, the surface ± puckered, of a medium green color, and nearly hairless, margins serrated, apex obtuse to pointed. Flowers (infrequently produced in Hawai'i) are in terminal headlike clusters 0.5–1 inch in diameter; the corollas are purple.

DISTRIBUTION: *Mentha aquatica* is native in Europe and western Asia, where it grows in wet fields and along the shores of ponds and banks of streams. It has a strong scent and is not one of the more popular mints in the West, yet it is preferred by Southeast Asians.

USE: In Southeast Asian cuisine, fresh mint leaves are used in preparing a variety of salads, hors d'oeuvres, and appetizers: they are shredded with *Polygonum odoratum* (q.v.) and served over steamed dumplings; incorporated into the filling for summer rolls; and as a garnish for spring rolls and mixed grill. The Thais and Laotians use whole mint leaves in raw beef salad *(laab).*

EXPOSURE: Full sun with liberal quantities of water or partial shade in dry situations. Under sunnier exposures the plants are more compact and bushy (i.e., they have shorter stem internodes), whereas in the shade the stems are more elongate and spindly, producing an untidy plant.

PROPAGATION METHODS:

Seed: Uncommon for home gardeners, although commercial herb growers use seed.

Cuttings: 4–6-inch stem-tip cuttings root rapidly in five to ten days in a 50:50 peat-perlite medium. Mint will also root quickly in water, but these water roots are more difficult to establish when transplanted to a soil medium.

Division: The plant tends to spread out along the ground and root as it grows. These lengthy pieces can be severed from the main plant and reestablished. When using this method, cut the plant back to the root zone or ground level to encourage new growth. New shoots will emerge from the creeping stems.

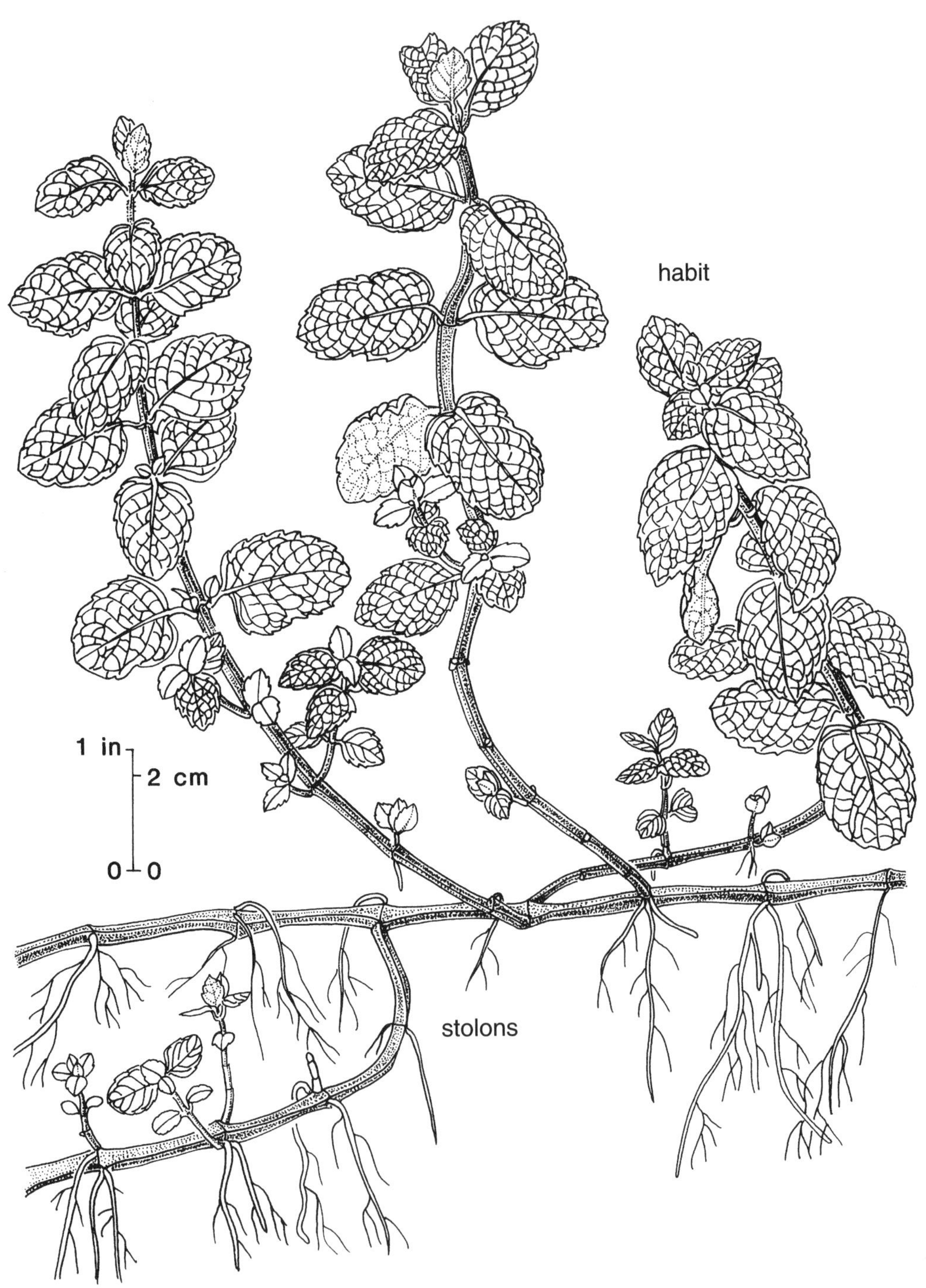

Mentha aquatica

CULTURAL PRACTICES: Mint grows prolifically, can be invasive, and should be contained in a large tub or similar container. Plant 6 inches apart in an organically rich soil and water well. Water mint likes moist conditions, and the more frequent the watering the faster it will grow. Frequent pruning will assure plentiful edible leaves and prevent the development of flowers. It tends to proliferate in the spring and summer and then deteriorate later in the season, at which time a hard cutting will stimulate fresh new growth. Mint is best replanted every other year and the old woody sections of the plant discarded. Alternatively, the entire plant can be cut down to ground level.

PESTS: The leaves are occasionally eaten by insects, but in many cases a general shabby appearance is caused by lack of water. Aphids, if numerous on new leaves, cause deformation and curling. The leaf miner is a common pest best controlled by pruning infected leaves. The affected leaves should be destroyed.

COMMENTS: Very fast growing.

Moringa oleifera Lamarck

Synonym: *Moringa pterygosperma* Gaertner

Moringaceae, the moringa family

COMMON NAMES: English: horseradish tree, drumstick tree; Japanese: *wasabi-no-ki;* Lao: *i houm;* Pilipino: *marungay, malunggay;* Thai: *marum;* Vietnamese: *ba dau dai, chum ngay.*

DESCRIPTION: Slender tree 10–35 feet tall, crown open and slender, wood soft, the bark corky. Leaves crowded toward the branch ends, petiole base swollen, blade 2–4×-pinnately compound, the leaflets ovate to oblong or obovate, 0.33–0.8 inch × 0.2–0.5 inch, medium green above, paler below. Flowers in terminal branched clusters, fragrant; sepals green, joined into a tube; petals white with greenish base, hairy on the basal part, curved to one side; stamens curved to one side, filaments hairy; ovary densely hairy; style hairless toward the apex. Fruit a pendent 3-valved capsule, 6–18 inches long, tan to brownish, ribbed lengthwise, opening explosively. Seeds ± rounded, pea sized, with 3 papery wings, the seed coat reticulate.

DISTRIBUTION: Native to northwestern India and now widespread throughout Asia and Africa as a result of cultivation. The tree is common in Hawai'i, especially around Filipino homesites.

USE: Virtually every part of this tree is useful. The seeds are the source of *ben oil,* used in artwork, precision machinery, and medicine. The grated root is used as a substitute for horseradish, which it greatly resembles in flavor. Young tender pods are eaten as a vegetable, and the fresh leaves are added to soups and stews for the spicy flavor they impart. Numerous Filipino dishes, such as boiled pork, fish, and chicken, as well as chicken or mung bean soup, are seasoned with the leaves. The mature, hardened seed pods are not eaten.

EXPOSURE: Full sun.

CULTIVATION: Usually kept severely pruned to assure a continuous supply of young leaves and to keep the edible parts within easy reach. Although it will reach 35 feet in height if left untrimmed, most cultivated *marungay* are much smaller; it could be grown in a greenhouse if kept cut back. It also presents possibilities for bonsai. Unfortunately, local pruning practices (cutting with cane knives, breaking branches by hand) often result in ugly-looking plants.

PROPAGATION METHODS:

Seed: The large seeds are easy to germinate and are best sown in individual pots; often, discarded styrofoam cups are used for this purpose by local gardeners, who poke

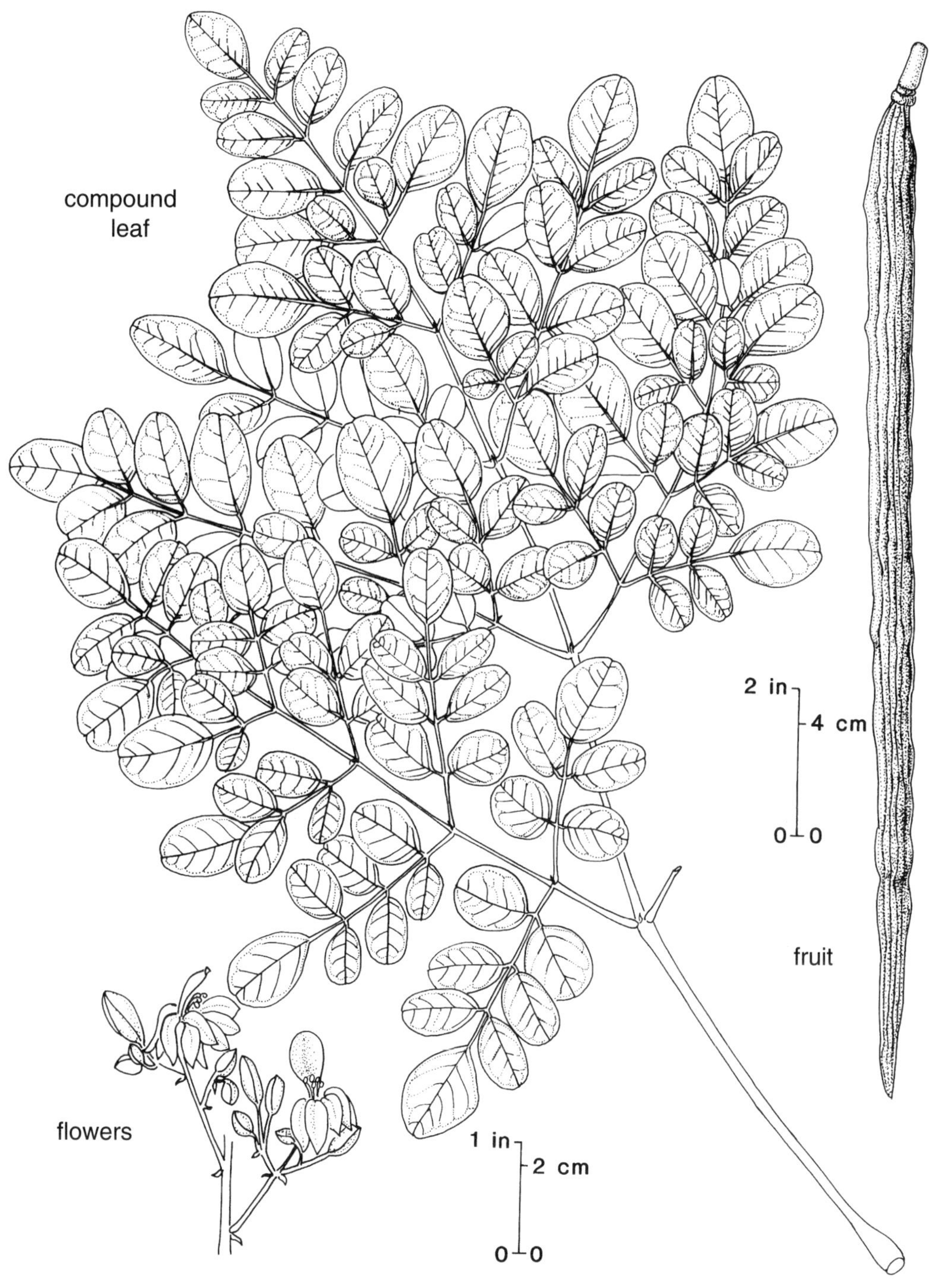

Moringa oleifera

drainage holes in the bottom of the cup before filling it with soil. A loamy soil is best, and when seedlings reach 6–8 inches tall they may be transplanted into the ground or a larger container.

Cuttings: Cuttings are rooted successfully in Hawai'i. This is best done by taking cuttings 6–8 inches long from semiripe (i.e., partially woody) stems, using a sharp cut below the lowest node. Strip off the leaves from the lower half of the cutting and place in a 50:50 peat-perlite rooting medium. Cuttings strike best with bottom heat.

Division: Not applicable.

PESTS: Mealy bugs and leaf miners attack the foliage, while cabbage butterfly *(Pieris* sp.*)* caterpillars chew the leaves. Spray regularly with 1 tablespoon of dish detergent in 1 gallon of water to deter these pests.

COMMENTS: Fast growing.

Murraya koenigii (Linnaeus) Sprengel

Synonym: *Bergera koenigii* Linnaeus

Rutaceae, the citrus family

COMMON NAMES: English: curry leaf tree; Lao: *dok kibe;* Thai: *hom kaek.*

DESCRIPTION: Deciduous tree 15–20 feet tall, with a sparse, open crown. Leaves alternate, odd pinnately compound, leaflets 11–21, oblong-lanceolate to ovate, curved, base oblique, margins serrate, the apex pointed. Flowers in terminal clusters, white, fragrant; petals 5, oblong-lanceolate; stamens 10, alternating long and short; ovary 2-celled; style short and thick. Fruit a blackish, oblong berry. Seeds 1 or 2 per fruit.

DISTRIBUTION: Widely distributed in the Indian subcontinent, Sri Lanka, Myanmar, throughout Southeast Asia, southern China, and Hainan Island. It is likely to be cultivated wherever there are populations of expatriate Indians or Sri Lankans living in tropical or subtropical climates.

USE: The fresh leaflets are commonly used in southern India and Sri Lanka to flavor curry, usually by cooking the leaflets in clarified butter (ghee) or the curry liquid and discarding them before serving. Marian Bell Fairchild, wife of plant explorer David Fairchild, used the leaflets to flavor French dressing, removing them before the dressing was poured over the salad; her dinner guests found the taste pleasing.

EXPOSURE: Thrives in partial shade to full sun.

CULTIVATION: A porous, well-drained soil of average fertility is all that is necessary. Annual application of a general garden fertilizer is beneficial. Pruning to shape the crown will encourage formation of a more attractive specimen.

PROPAGATION METHODS:

Seed: Propagated readily from seed, which is abundantly produced. Clean seeds and remove fruit pulp before planting. Cover the seed to the depth of the size of the seed and water thoroughly. When seed has germinated and the seedlings have two sets of leaves, plant out into individual 3–4-inch pots.

Cuttings: Can be propagated by tip and stem cuttings if the tips are crisp and supple. These are best inserted in a 75:25 peat-perlite medium. Water only to keep the medium moist. These types of cuttings are slow.

Division: Root suckers develop from which new plants can be established. Locate the root from which the sucker emerges. A section of root 2–3 inches on either side of

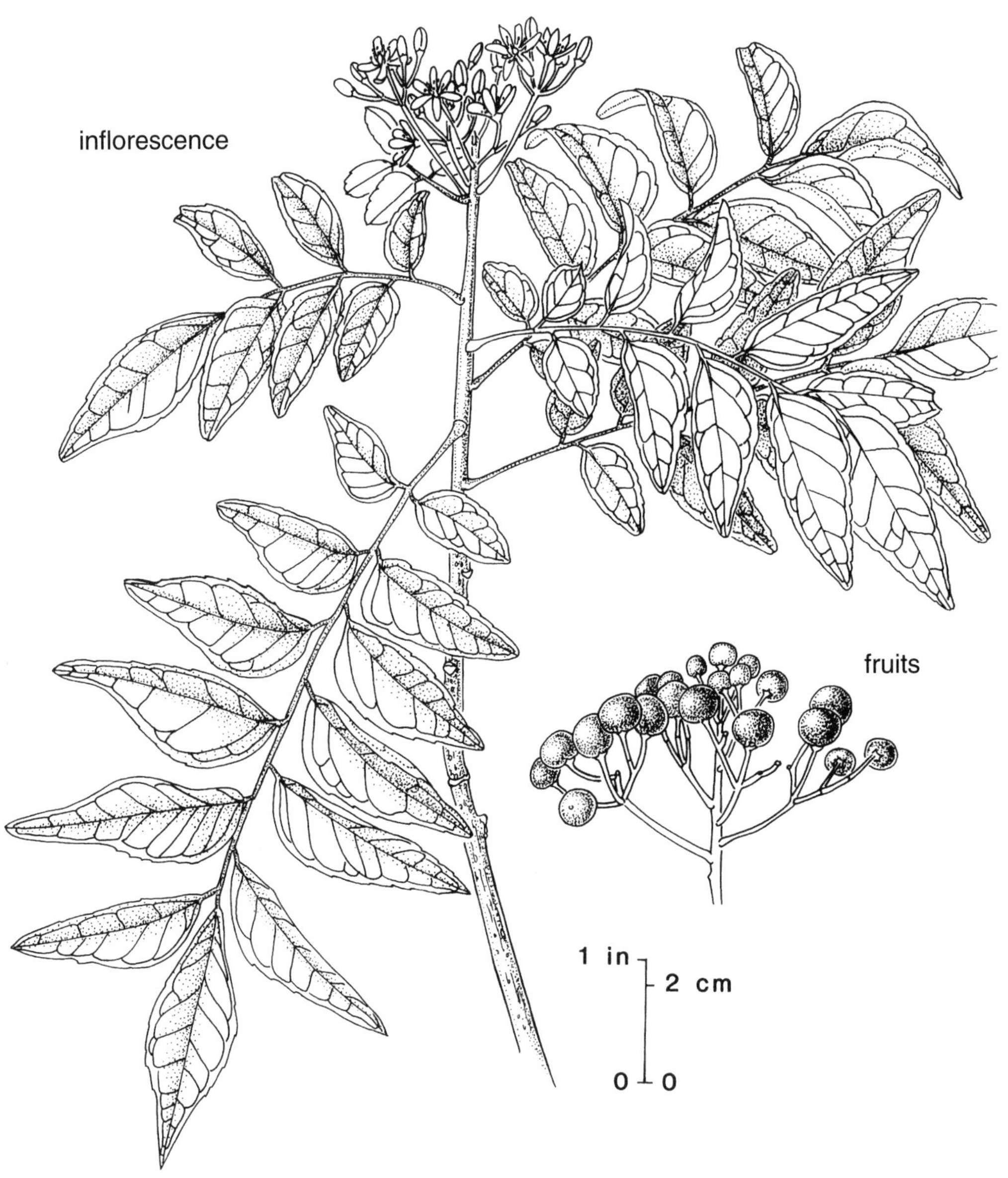

Murraya koenigii

the sucker can be cut off and replanted in a container, where an independent root system will develop.

CULTURAL PRACTICES: A typical small, under-canopy tree, the curry leaf tree is sparse in growth and leafless for short periods in the hot season. It is a low-maintenance tree that will benefit from pinching to induce a bushier, fuller crown. The soil should not be allowed to dry out.

PESTS: Whiteflies may be seasonally troublesome and can weaken plants. Spray weekly with 1 tablespoon detergent in 1 gallon water to deter this pest.

COMMENTS: This small, attractive tree should be excellent as a container plant and could have potential as a bonsai. Slow growing.

Ocimum basilicum Linnaeus

Lamiaceae (or Labiatae), the mint family

COMMON NAMES: English: sweet basil (general), anise-scented basil, Thai basil; Chinese: *ue heung;* Japanese: *me boki;* Pilipino: *balanoi, bidai;* Thai: *horaphaa;* Vietnamese: *cay ich gioi, chi sa, e tia, eque, hathuong, hung gioi, hung que, pak bua le phe, rau e, rau que, thaokai, ytou.*

DESCRIPTION: Perennial herb becoming woody at the base, forming mounds to 3 feet tall and as broad, all parts intensely fragrant; stems squarish, purple-tinged when young. Leaves opposite, petiole 0.33–0.75 inch long, blade ovate to elliptic, 1.25–2.5 inches × 0.75–1 inch, margins varying from smooth to irregularly serrate or frilled, surface medium green, often creased or wrinkled, base wedge-shaped, apex pointed; veins usually purplish-tinged. Inflorescence a terminal raceme or panicle, the stems and bracts purple. Flowers fragrant, usually 6 per whorl, the whorls often widely spaced along the main stem of the inflorescence; calyx dark purple with a ring of hairs inside; corolla whitish to pale pinkish purple. Fruit a dryish capsule enclosed in the slightly enlarged calyx, dehiscing to release the black, ellipsoidal nutlets, which become mucilaginous when wetted.

DISTRIBUTION: Widely distributed in the Old World tropics and now cultivated the world over as an herb and ornamental. In the tropics the plants are perennial, but in temperate zones they are usually grown as annuals. Many cultivars of sweet basil exist; the foregoing description refers to the purple-bracted form favored by Thai and Southeast Asian gardeners that is so abundant locally.

USE: The stem tips with tender young leaves and immature inflorescences are served fresh as a garnish for spring rolls, many kinds of Vietnamese soup *(pho,* etc.*),* and in many appetizers, and the leaves are also cooked in Thai stir-fry dishes. The leaves can be substituted in some recipes calling for Italian (sweet) basil, if the cook is adventuresome! The seeds are soaked in water and incorporated into Thai desserts, often in combination with the leaves of *Pandanus amaryllifolius* (q.v.) for fragrance. The chemical constituent *methyl chavicol* contributes the distinctive flavor to Thai basil. Most people identify this as an anise flavor; actually, it is nearer to tarragon.

EXPOSURE: Basil thrives in full sun as long as adequate water is provided. Plants may also be grown in partial shade, although insect infestation seems to be more of a problem under shady conditions. Plants tend to develop soft, weak growth under shady conditions, making them more susceptible to pests.

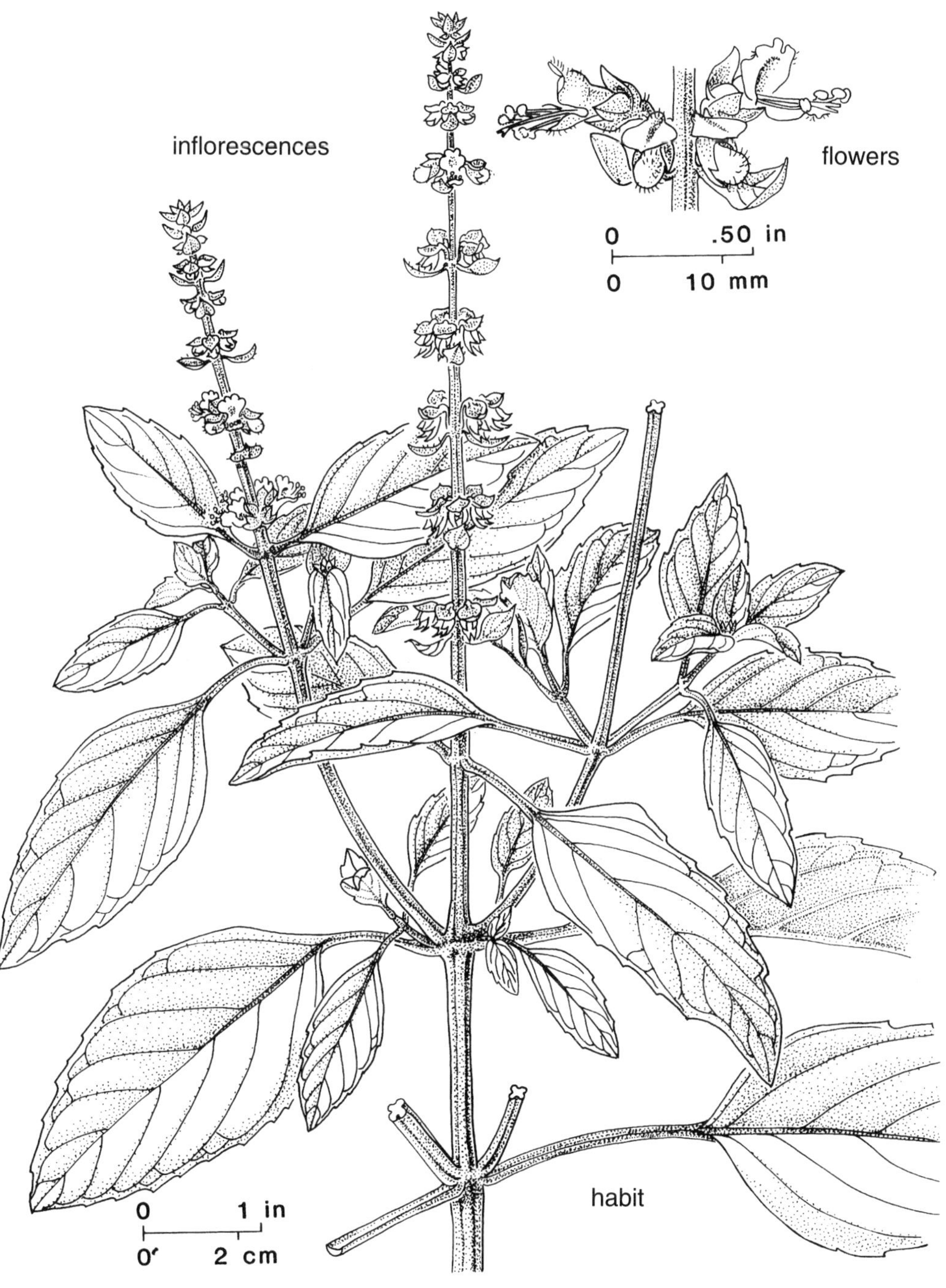

Ocimum basilicum

CULTIVATION: The plants need to be pinched back often to prevent flowers from forming and to stimulate side branching. The flavor of the leaves changes once flower buds develop; therefore the elimination of inflorescences is necessary to maintain an adequate supply of young leaves for culinary use.

PROPAGATION METHODS:

Seed: Seeds are seldom used in Hawai'i because this basil roots so readily from cuttings. Should seed be tried, make sure it comes from a reliable source (to assure that the cultivar comes true to type), sow the seed in a bed of fine loamy medium, just covering it with a thin layer, and mist or spray with a fine sprinkling head. Keep the seedbed in the sun and transplant the seedlings when they reach a height of 1 inch. Keep the new transplants shaded for a day or two before exposing them to full sun. Water thoroughly after planting.

Cuttings: Tip and stem cuttings are rapid and will strike roots in most media—even water. Tip cuttings 4–6 inches long strike roots in five to ten days in a 50:50 peat-perlite medium; bottom heat provides the best results. Set out into the garden as soon as the roots are established or when two sets of new leaves have developed.

Division: Not applicable.

CULTURAL PRACTICES: Basil grows rapidly and will develop into stronger plants if pinched or harvested continuously. Plant a minimum of 18 inches apart. In tropical and subtropical climates, basil tends to become rank and unsightly. The more frequently plants are pinched and pruned the faster they generate new fresh growth. Do not cut back to the woody base of the plant—no buds will break from this area and the plant will die. New plants are best established each year and old plants discarded. Remove the flower spikes as they develop to retain the leaves in the best condition.

PESTS: The leaf miner can become a menace; remove the affected leaves at the first sign of the tell-tale trails in the leaf blades. Thrips cause many commercial shipments of locally grown basil to be rejected when they reach the mainland. Mealy bugs can be a problem, as are aphids; these can be rinsed off with a strong stream of water from a garden hose. Whiteflies and fungi in damp, humid areas can affect Thai basil; careful choice of planting location is the best preventative for these problems. Spittle bug foam is often found in the leaf axils near the stem tips; this is easily washed out with a spray of water. Spraying with detergent water (1 tablespoon per gallon) will kill the spittle bug.

COMMENTS: Grows rapidly and therefore usually treated as an annual in the tropics.

Ocimum tenuiflorum Linnaeus

Synonym: *Ocimum sanctum* Linnaeus

Lamiaceae (or Labiatae), the mint family

COMMON NAMES: English: holy basil; Pilipino: *bidai, sulasi;* Thai: *kha phrao, kha phrao khaao, kha phrao daeng;* Vietnamese: *che tak me, e do, erung, e tia.*

DESCRIPTION: Perennial herb becoming woody at the base; stems squarish when young. Leaves opposite, petiole 0.2–0.6 inch long, blade oblong to narrowly ovate, obtuse or rounded at both ends, margins undulate; veins often reddish- or purplish-tinged. Inflorescence a simple raceme (rarely branched at the base), flowers usually 6 per whorl, the whorls rather closely spaced; calyx purplish or greenish, glabrous inside; corolla reddish pink, sometimes almost whitish. Fruit enclosed in the persistent calyx. Nutlets brownish, warty, not mucilaginous when wetted.

Holy basil is easy to recognize because the old inflorescence stalks persist on the plants after the flowers and fruits have fallen off. The stalks—bearing short, down-curved pedicels—have a distinctive appearance that is unmistakable once recognized. The leaf shape is also characteristic: an oblong or lozenge-shaped blade that may come in either a purplish or green color form.

DISTRIBUTION: Native throughout the Old World tropics and now widespread as a cultivated herb and an escaped weed.

USE: In India, the clove-scented leaves are considered holy by Hindus and are used in religious ceremonies. The Thais use fresh holy basil in stir-fry dishes, often in combination with searingly hot chili peppers and lots of onions or shallots, to produce a flavor combination that is both hot and aromatic. Holy basil is also popular in making basil jelly and as a flavoring for fruit dishes, breads, potpourris, and sachets. One of the major chemical constituents in *O. tenuiflorum* is eugenol, which contributes to its distinctive flavor/aroma.

EXPOSURE: Full sun is best, provided water is ample; plants will also grow in partial shade. Holy basil will tolerate less water than *O. basilicum,* and some people feel that plants grown under drier conditions produce more intensely fragrant leaves.

PROPAGATION METHODS:

Seed: Germinates readily, although seed is seldom used in Hawai'i because cuttings strike so readily.

Cuttings: Tip and stem cuttings root rapidly and will strike in most rooting media—even water. These strike in seven to fourteen days in a 50:50 peat-perlite medium; bottom heat produces better results with this medium. Set out into the

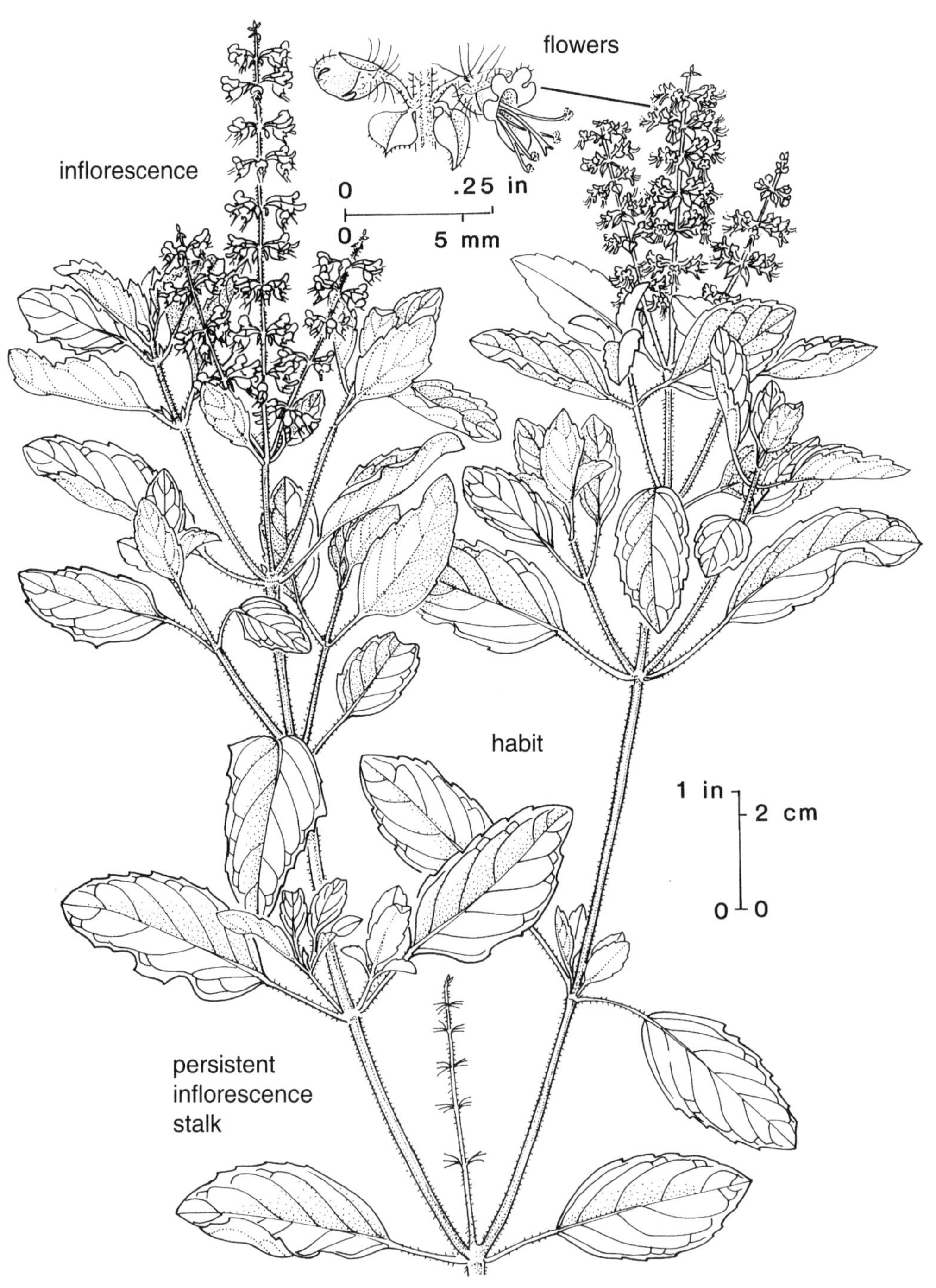

Ocimum tenuiflorum

garden as soon as the roots are established or when two sets of new leaves have been produced.

CULTURAL PRACTICES: Holy basil grows rapidly and will develop into a stronger plant if pinched or harvested continuously. Plant a minimum of 18 inches apart. Holy basil is a short-lived perennial under tropical conditions, lasting two or three years before needing replacement. Seeds are abundantly produced and volunteer seedlings can become weedy pests in the garden. The more frequently they are pinched and pruned the faster they generate new, fresh growth. As with sweet basil, prune only softwood and do not cut back to the woody base or the plant will die. Remove the flower spikes as they develop to retain the leaves in the best condition.

PESTS: The leaf miner tends to become a problem in the fall. By removing leaves at the first signs of leaf damage, this pest may be controlled. Fruit flies are attracted to the flower spikes, and some gardeners grow holy basil near mango or other fruit trees in the belief that fruit flies will be attracted to the basil and leave the fruit alone.

COMMENTS: Grows rapidly and therefore often grown as an annual in the tropics.

Pandanus amaryllifolius Roxburgh

Synonyms: *Pandanus latifolius* Hasskarl, *P. odorus* Ridley

Pandanaceae, the screw-pine family

COMMON NAMES: English: dwarf screw pine, dwarf *pandan,* fragrant screw pine; Malay: *pandan wangi, pandan rampai;* Pilipino: *pandan, pandan-mabango;* Thai: *bai toey, paanae wo-nging, toey hom;* Vietnamese: *dua thom.*

DESCRIPTION: A shrubby perennial that sprawls along the ground with the tips upturned or may half climb if supported. Stem as thick as a finger or less, producing aerial roots from the nodes, reaching 5–6 feet long if untrimmed. Leaves spirally arranged, linear to lance-shaped, 12–18 inches long and 1–1.5 inches wide, pleated lengthwise parallel to the midrib, spineless except at the apex where a few minute prickles are produced on the margins and on the underside of the midrib, glabrous, upper surface shiny pale to medium green, underside glaucous whitish. Flowers and fruits unknown and seemingly never produced in cultivation.

DISTRIBUTION: Probably native to the Molucca Islands and cultivated since antiquity in Malaysia, throughout Indonesia, Thailand, Vietnam, the Philippines, Sri Lanka, and possibly in Taiwan.

USE: The leaves, either whole or finely cut up, are cooked with rice and other foods, principally sweets in Thailand and Vietnam, to which they impart a distinctive fragrance; also used in floral arrangements and to make fragrant water used in religious ceremonies. Some people find the musky, sweet odor of the cut leaves overpowering.

EXPOSURE: Full sun or partial shade, though pests are more prevalent in shady settings.

PROPAGATION METHODS:

Seed: Flowers and fruits are unknown, so all propagation is vegetative.

Cuttings: Tip cuttings root easily in a shady, well-drained medium such as perlite or clean washed sand. Cuttings will root in water, although brittle, easily damaged roots result. Cuttings are slow and care must be taken not to allow water to accumulate in the crown of leaves, where rot might develop. Harden off into bright light, then into full sun.

Division: A single plant proliferates into a sizable clump through production of side shoots and plantlets near the base. Division of these clumps is one easy means to increase the number of plants. In the case of a side branch, cut off the shoot tip above

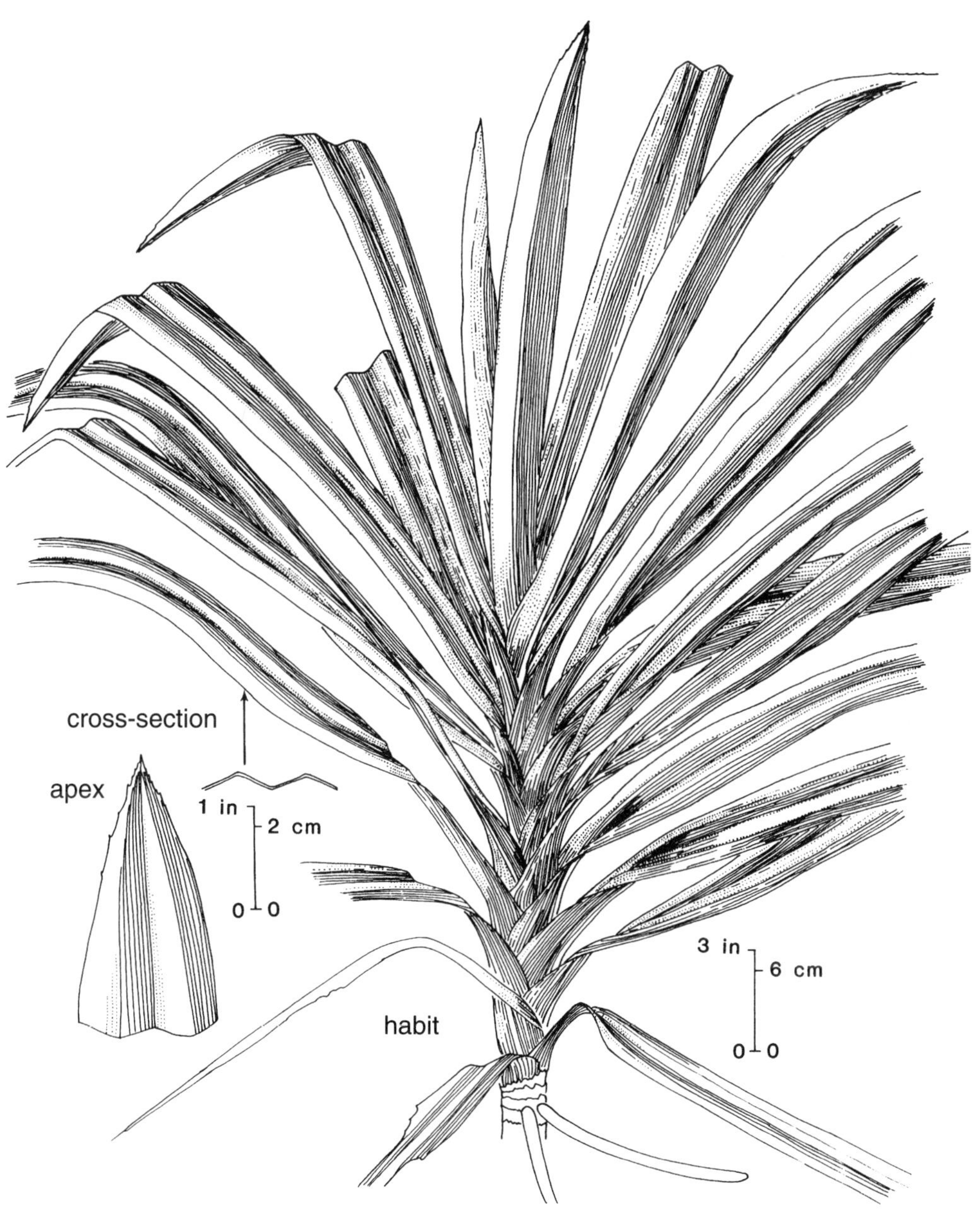

Pandanus amaryllifolius

the side branch and root as a cutting; the side branch will then become a new leader. Or wait until adventitious roots form at the base of the side branch and remove it as a vegetative plantlet. Such plantlets can be planted directly into soil in a pot, where fibrous roots will soon develop.

CULTURAL PRACTICES: Plant out into well-drained soil at least 3 feet apart to allow space for the clumping habit. One plant is adequate for home use. As an ornamental, dwarf *pandan* is an excellent textural plant for the garden but needs ample space in which to grow. Grown outdoors in the Hawaiian climate, one plant will develop a 15-foot spread over several years if allowed to develop without pruning. Dwarf *pandan* is considered a low-maintenance plant that can be neglected for years, although the continual vegetative suckering will ultimately produce an untidy clump of vegetation. Periodically remove lower leaves that turn brown; fertilize every three months with a balanced plant food, and mulch to a depth of 3 inches.

PESTS: Red spider mites and mealy bugs can be problems in shady, humid, protected situations. In bright sun with good air circulation, pests are seldom a problem.

COMMENTS: Moderately fast growing once established.

Peperomia pellucida (Linnaeus) Kunth

Piperaceae, the pepper family

COMMON NAMES: English: peperomia; Pilipino: *sahica-puti, ulasimanbato;* Thai: *kasang pak, phak krasang;* Vietnamese: *rau cangcua.*

DESCRIPTION: Small glabrous herb with fibrous roots; stems translucent greenish and semisucculent. Leaves alternate, petiole 0.25–1.2 inches long, blade ovate, 0.5–2 inches × 0.33–1.25 inches, pale to medium green above, whitish on the underside, margin entire (smooth), venation 3- or 5- palmate. Inflorescence a threadlike spike, either terminal or opposite a leaf, 1.2–2.25 inches long. Fruit a subglobose berry with longitudinal ridges, ca. 0.125 inch in diameter, the apex beaked.

DISTRIBUTION: Native to the American tropics but widely cultivated and naturalized elsewhere. A common weed in greenhouses and nurseries, it has been speculated that this peperomia has been carried along in the soil when potted plants are transported and has thus been widely distributed outside its natural range. *Peperomia pellucida* is naturalized in Hawai'i and seems to be sparingly cultivated as well.

USE: This plant is sometimes to be found for sale in Vietnamese and Southeast Asian markets in Honolulu. Whether it is cultivated or collected from weedy populations is unclear. Filipinos eat it in green salad. In Thailand the young shoots and stems are blanched and eaten with *nam phrik* or *laab.* In Indonesia and the Philippines it is used medicinally.

EXPOSURE: Shady and damp, either in soil or gravel, or as an epiphyte.

PROPAGATION METHODS:

Seed: Rarely propagated from seed, *Peperomia pellucida* seeds itself freely in moist, shady conditions.

Cuttings: Easily propagated by tip and stem cuttings inserted in a 75:25 peat-vermiculite mixture. Cuttings 4–6 inches long quickly produce a mass of roots in moist conditions with good drainage. Because the stems are brittle, it is best to make a hole first, then insert the cutting and firm the medium around it so the fragile stems are not broken in handling. As soon as roots develop, pot up or plant out.

Division: Not applicable.

CULTURAL PRACTICES: Plant 8 inches apart in a fibrous organic medium. Because *P. pellucida* grows so readily in damp gravel on greenhouse benches or floors, it would be interesting to try cultivating it in pots using gravel or sand as a

Peperomia pellucida

medium and fertilizing with weak water-soluble fertilizer. Water liberally. Pinch the stem tips to encourage side branching. If the peperomia receives too much water, it can develop edema. The succulent nature of the plant tends to retain excessive moisture under high humidity. This is a lush green plant that is a good filler to offset less attractive herbs.

PESTS: None observed.

COMMENTS: Very fast growing and can become weedy.

Perilla frutescens (Linnaeus) Britton

Lamiaceae (or Labiatae), the mint family

COMMON NAMES: English: beefsteak plant, perilla; Chinese: *bai su zi, zi-su;* Japanese: *shiso, chiso;* Thai: *ngaa khee mon* (northern dialect); Vietnamese: *cay tia to, tia to.*

DESCRIPTION: Coarse perennial herb 3–5 feet tall; stems squarish, becoming woody at the base; all parts fragrant when bruised. Leaves opposite, petiolate, blade ovate, 2.75–5 inches × 2–3.25 inches, flat or curly, deep green or purple in color, margins toothed. Flowers tiny (ca. 0.1 inch long), in terminal or axillary racemes; calyx bell shaped and 5-toothed; corolla white to reddish, tubular at the base, unequally 5-lobed above; stamens with free filaments. Fruits 4 tiny nutlets enclosed in swollen calyx up to 0.5 inch long.

DISTRIBUTION: Widely distributed in Asia from India to Japan, this species is quite variable and several infraspecific taxa have been named. *Perilla frutescens* 'Crispa' is the cultivar most often cultivated in North America.

USE: The Japanese use the fresh leaves as a spice for bean curd and raw fish (sashimi); the leaves and flower spikes are used in salads, soups, or for tempura. The Japanese traditionally used the purple-leaved *shiso* to color preserved apricots, young pickled ginger, and tubers of Japanese artichoke *(Stachys sieboldii* Miquel*)*. The Vietnamese use the fresh leaves as a salad herb and for garnishes. American restaurants featuring nouvelle cuisine often use *chiso* leaves as garnishes for dinner plates and serving dishes.

Many medicinal uses exist for perilla in southeastern Asia. Prolonged contact with *shiso* produces contact dermatitis in some people. An oil—*yegoma* or perilla oil—expressed from the seeds is used much like linseed oil. In Japan, for example, traditional paper umbrellas are waterproofed with perilla oil; *e-goma* is the Japanese name for cultivars selected for seed oil production. Wild forms of *P. frutescens* are toxic due to ketones present in the stems and leaves. Horticultural selection over a long period of time has produced cultivars without these perilla ketones, which are powerful respiratory toxins.

EXPOSURE: Shade or partial to full sun, as long as ample water is provided.

PROPAGATION METHODS:

Seed: Usually grown from locally packaged seeds, readily available in garden shops and nurseries. Alternatively, seedlings that volunteer in the garden near mature plants

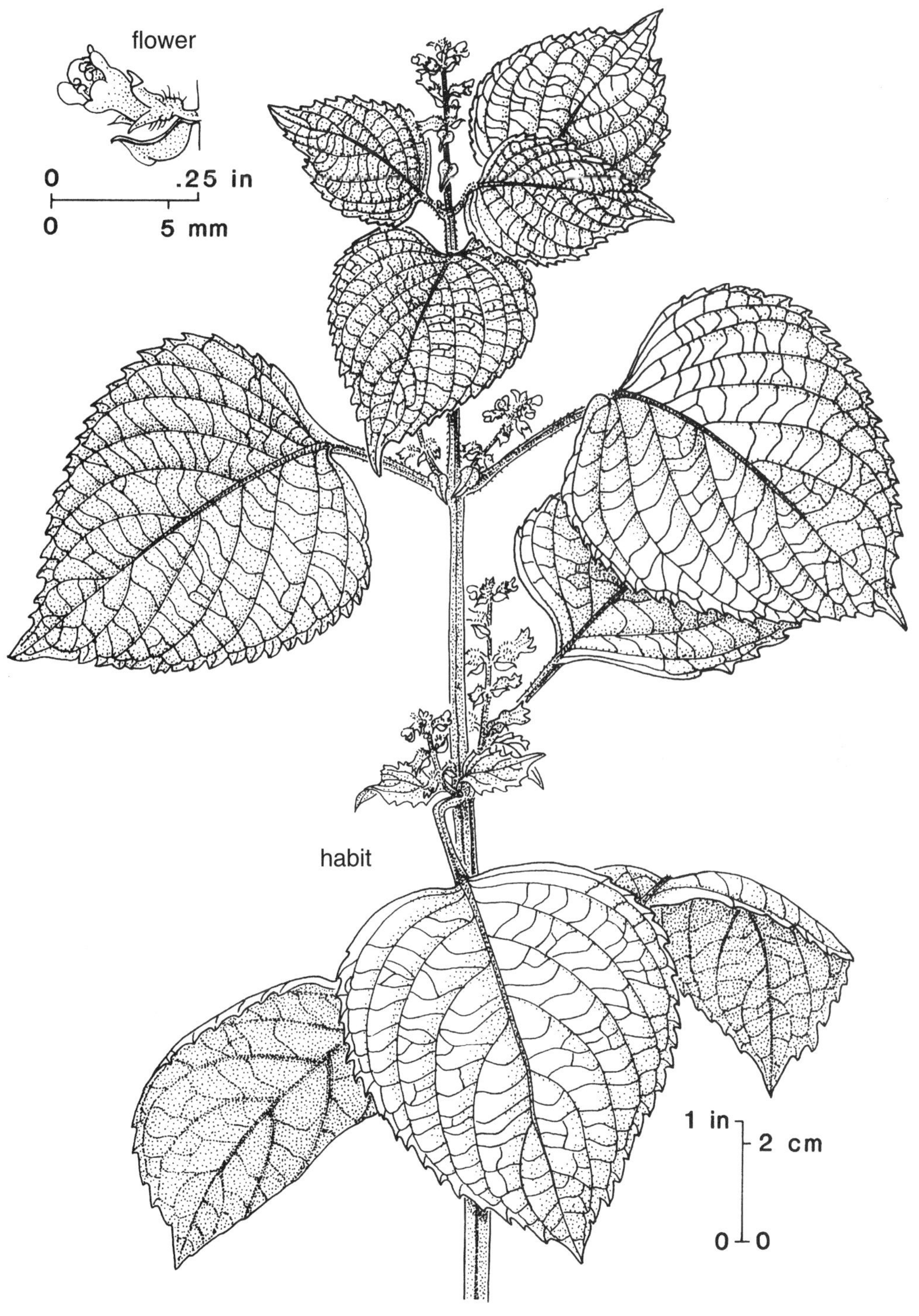

Perilla frutescens

may be lifted and transplanted into beds. Many local gardeners propagate their plants in this way.

Cuttings: Easily started by tip and stem cutting. Cut lengths 4–6 inches below the node and insert in a 50:50 peat-perlite medium. These strike root in five to ten days.

Division: Not applicable.

CULTURAL PRACTICES: Perilla is considered a high-maintenance herb because its rapid growth rate tends to produce a tall, slender plant without side branches. Repeatedly pinching out inflorescences as soon as they appear stimulates side branching and keeps the plant in vigorous vegetative growth.

The preferred soil is moisture retaining, organically rich, and well drained. Before planting, the soil should be dug to a depth of 12 inches and amended with one-third its volume in humus. When planted out, seedlings should be spaced 24 inches apart and shaded until they have hardened off. Plants reach about 3–5 feet in height and become very scraggly if they suffer infrequent watering: The lower leaves drop and leaf margins turn brown and curl. Pinching shoot tips tends to stimulate branching and produces a more attractive looking plant. Perilla is best grown as an annual, discarding plants after one year.

PESTS: Whiteflies. Spray weekly with detergent solution (1 tablespoon per gallon) until problem disappears.

COMMENTS: Grows rapidly.

Piper lolot C. deCandolle
Piperaceae, the pepper family

COMMON NAMES: English: *lolot;* Vietnamese: *la lat, la lot, lo lot.*

DESCRIPTION: Low-growing perennial herb, spreading by underground rhizomes, erect stems 6–10 inches tall, brownish. Leaf petiole up to 1 inch long, with a sheathing base, blade ovate, 3.5–5 inches × 2.5–3.25 inches, base cordate and symmetrical, margin entire, texture thin and membranous, upper surface puckered and glabrous, glossy deep green, underside finely hairy along the veins, otherwise glabrous, duller colored; 2 main secondary veins emerging from the midvein above the base and 3 or 4 other lateral nerves emerging above them, the outermost arching and diverging more than the others. Inflorescence a club-shaped spike up to 0.5 inch long, creamy white; flowers unisexual; pistillate flowers sunk into the inflorescence axis and partially fused with it, stigmas 3, linear. Fruits not produced.

DISTRIBUTION: Native to Southeast Asia in Vietnam, Cambodia, and Laos. *Lolot* is now cultivated in many tropical areas where Vietnamese immigrants have settled.

USE: The leaves are used to impart a delicate flavor to roast beef or *satay,* an Asian version of shish kebab: fresh leaves are dipped in boiling water to keep them from burning, then wrapped around small pieces of beef, secured with a toothpick, and placed on a skewer for grilling. It can also be eaten fresh, stuffed with chopped nuts and meats. The glossy leaves are used as an attractive garnish for plates and serving bowls.

EXPOSURE: Semishade if grown under drier conditions or full sun if the soil never dries out.

PROPAGATION METHODS:

Seed: Not applicable.

Cuttings: Prepare tip and stem cuttings 4–6 inches long, cutting off the upper half of the leaf blades; this reduces water loss due to transpiration and promotes more effective rooting. Insert the cuttings into a 50:50 peat-perlite medium, water well, and keep shaded. Strong clusters of roots typically form within fourteen days over bottom heat.

Division: *Lolot* forms abundant underground runners, eventually forming a tangled clump of plants. It is possible to divide mature clumps and sever underground runners with roots from the main plant. Lift a clump with a spading fork, then cut

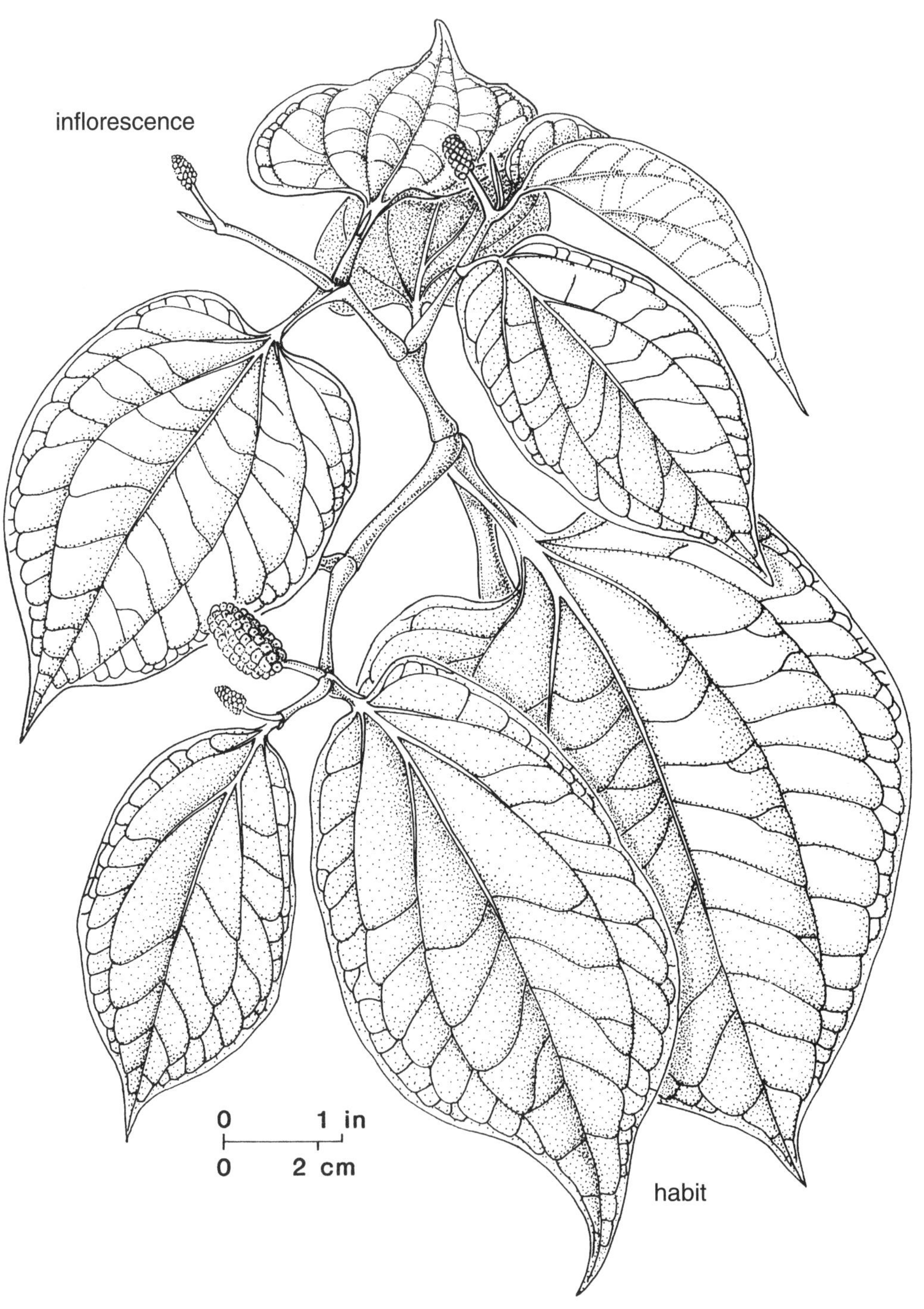
inflorescence
0 1 in
0 2 cm
habit

Piper lolot

with a sharp knife or spade. These divisions can be planted directly into a loam soil and watered thoroughly. Water sparingly after that until signs of new growth appear. Alternatively, 6-inch lengths of unrooted runner material can be lifted, cleaned, and inserted as cuttings. These will readily root and soon produce above-ground stems and leaves.

CULTURAL PRACTICES: *Lolot* develops into a beautiful emerald green plant that makes an attractive groundcover or container plant. Unfortunately, under tropical conditions it can be invasive, so it is best grown in large pots or confined within a sunken border to prevent underground spread. A space 5 feet in diameter will allow *lolot* to develop its full potential. Pinch the shoot tips to prevent flowering and stimulate fresh leaf growth. Established plants require thinning of dense inner stems to allow free air circulation into the center of the clump and stimulate new shoots from the runners.

PESTS: Chlorosis of the leaves, often manifested as yellow blotches on the green leaf, is common in Hawai'i. The cause is unknown.

COMMENTS: Rapid growing once established.

Plectranthus amboinicus (Loureiro) Sprengel

Synonym: *Coleus amboinicus* Loureiro

Lamiaceae (or Labiatae), the mint family

COMMON NAMES: English: Greek oregano, Spanish thyme, false oregano; Portuguese: oregano; Malay: *daun bangun-bangun;* Pilipino: *suganda;* Thai: *hom duan huu suea, niam huu suea;* Vietnamese: *can day la, rau cang, rau thom lun.*

DESCRIPTION: A mound-forming succulent perennial herb, up to 5 feet in diameter and about 3 feet tall if left untrimmed, intensely scented like oregano. The square stems sprawl along the ground and turn upward at the tips, becoming woody when older; younger ones firm-fleshy. Leaves opposite, petiolate, blades thick and firm-fleshy in texture, rather brittle and easily broken, ovate in outline, margins toothed, apex obtuse to acute, hairy on both sides. Inflorescence a simple (rarely with 1 or 2 branches at the base) terminal spike of crowded whorls, each whorl containing 4–10 sessile flowers, densely hairy; corolla lilac, mauve, or whitish, tube slightly bent near the middle, the upper lip erect, with 2 lateral earlike lobes, the lower lip horizontal and boat-shaped.

DISTRIBUTION: Many contradictory statements are made in the botanical and horticultural literature regarding the original home of this species. According to a taxonomic revision of the genus *Plectranthus* in South Africa, it is probably native to tropical Africa from whence it was carried to India and Southeast Asia by the Arabs and Portuguese, later to Europe, and from there to the New World. The common name *Spanish thyme* originated in the Americas, where *P. amboinicus* was introduced from Spain. How it reached Hawai'i—and from where—is unknown.

USE: The leaves are generally used fresh, either whole or finely diced as a substitute for oregano in flavoring soups, stews, sauces; it is particularly useful in masking strong odors and flavors such as those of fish, mutton, and goat. In Cuba it is used as an integral seasoning for *frijoles negros,* the national black bean soup. Virtually every kitchen garden in Latin America has a plant, so it is seldom seen for sale in rural markets. The Vietnamese use the leaves in meat dishes and stews and in India the leaves are fried in batter. *Plectranthus amboinicus* has a variety of medicinal uses.

EXPOSURE: Full sun; this species thrives in dry, sunny locations. When grown under shady or partly shady conditions, it becomes scraggly and unattractive.

PROPAGATION METHODS:
Seed: Rarely grown from seed because the plants seldom flower and set seed.

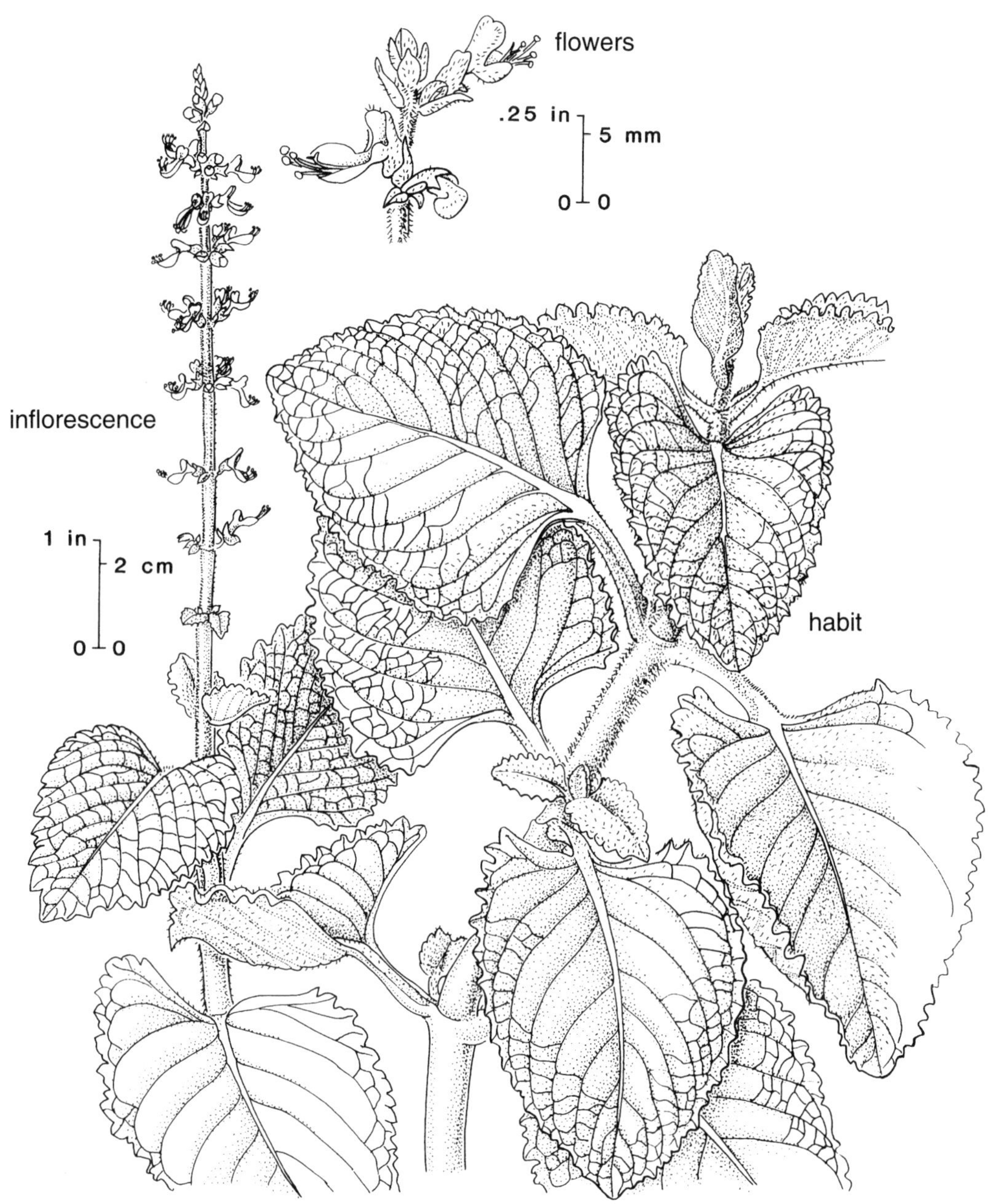

Plectranthus amboinicus

Cuttings: Tip or stem cuttings 6–8 inches in length strike root easily. The most efficient method is to make a clean cut below a node and remove the leaves from the three nodes above the cut. Insert at least 4 inches into washed sand, fine-grade perlite, or a 50:50 peat-perlite mixture. Firm the cuttings and water thoroughly. Rooting takes place in seven to ten days with bottom heat; without bottom heat, the roots take longer to form but still yield good results. Cuttings are best started in a shady location. As the plant becomes established and roots develop, the amount of sunlight is increased. Pinching the shoot tip induces a stronger plant and reduces its sprawling habit.

Division: Although Greek oregano does not produce a compound root and stem structure suitable for division, it is possible to divide mature clumps of tangled stems and obtain rooted material suitable for replanting or stem material suitable for cuttings.

CULTIVATION: Since Greek oregano tends to be a fast and rank grower, it will soon become pot-bound; therefore, once a strong root mass has formed the plant should be planted out immediately. Plant at least 3–5 feet apart in full sun. A mature plant develops within twelve months, and because of its rapid growth rate Greek oregano could be considered high maintenance. As the plant develops the lower stems become leafless and woody and hence unattractive. Regular pruning will counteract this tendency by encouraging vigorous new shoots. After three to five years, a mature plant is best replaced with a young one started from the parent. Greek oregano is an attractive ornamental when grown in a sunny location. A cultivar with variegated leaves, prettily marked with white margins and a pink blush, is available in the trade.

PESTS: Mealy bugs and aphids occasionally attack the foliage. Spray with 1 tablespoon dish soap per gallon of water in late afternoon. Increase sprayings if the problem persists. Do not spray in hot, sunny weather as this may cause burning of the foliage, manifested as brown spots on the leaves. Damping-off fungus may kill young plants grown under humid, damp conditions.

COMMENTS: Grows rapidly.

Polygonum odoratum Loureiro
Polygonaceae, the buckwheat family

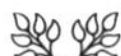

COMMON NAMES: English: fragrant knotweed; Thai: *phak phai;* Vietnamese: *nghe, rau ram.*

DESCRIPTION: A sprawling annual herb with reddish stems that turn up at the tips; roots form freely from the nodes. All parts of the plant are fragrant when bruised. Leaves are alternate and have a distinctive sheath where the petiole joins the stem. The blade is lanceolate, margins entire (not toothed), medium to bright green, often with a darker green or purplish blotch in the lower middle area, and almost hairless. Flowers are rarely produced, usually only if the nights are cool and plant has not been pruned or pinched back. The inflorescence is a simple spike, the flowers are small and pink, with 5 petals and 3 stamens. Fruits have not been documented and may never form.

DISTRIBUTION: Native to Southeast Asia and probably cultivated in Malaysia, Vietnam, Thailand, Laos, and Cambodia under a variety of different scientific names. While it is not certain that all these variously named plants are the same species, it seems likely that they are. In English the common names *smartweed* or *knotweed* are generally used for *Polygonum* species. Fragrant knotweed is suggested as a common name in English for this Asian species that is new to cultivation in the United States.

USE: The aromatic fresh leaves are shredded with mint and served as a garnish for steamed dumplings *(cheong fun),* used in salads, and eaten whole with spring rolls. It is said that the leaves are never cooked; only fresh leaves are used. The odor is like that of coriander with a lemon tang, and the flavor is peppery and lemony at the same time. Some have characterized the flavor as "soapy." The leaves are also used to garnish meat or fowl and are eaten with fertilized duck eggs. The leaves are also pickled with other ingredients in a sauerkraut-like dish called *dua can.* A number of folk medicinal uses are known from Southeast Asia.

EXPOSURE: Semishade is best for growing this species unless abundant moisture is provided, in which case full sun is tolerated.

PROPAGATION METHODS:

Seed: Unknown.

Cuttings: Easily propagated by tip and stem cuttings 3–4 inches long: Cut below the node, remove the lower leaves, and insert in pure peat moss or in a 50:50 peat-

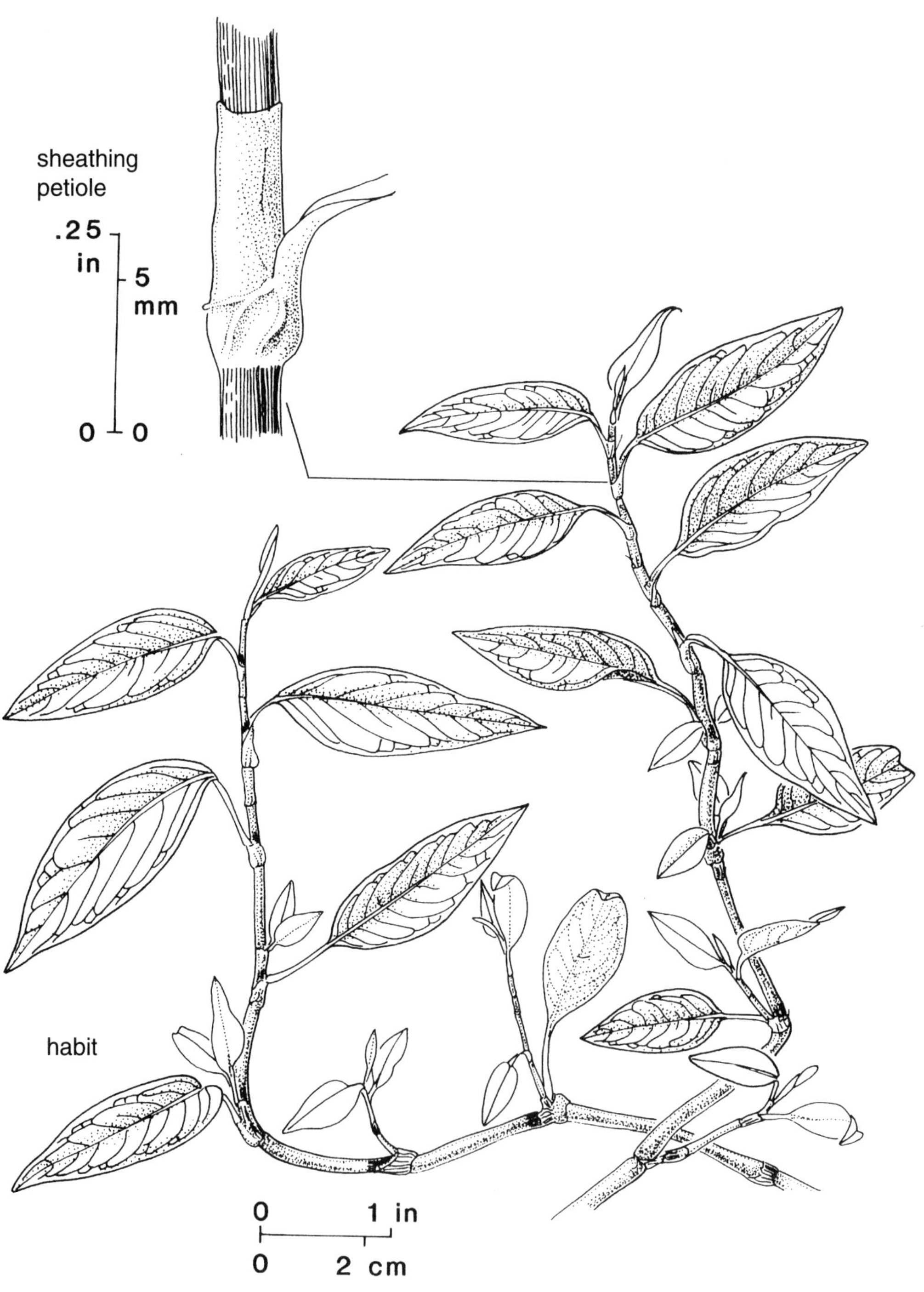

Polygonum odoratum

perlite medium. Keep moist and well shaded; roots form in seven to fourteen days with bottom heat.

Division: The plant develops a compound crown of a dense clump of stems. This crown can be divided by inserting a sharp knife into the center, cutting through the crown, and dividing it.

CULTURAL PRACTICES: Plants require an organically rich, moist soil and should be set out 18 inches apart to allow for the sprawling habit. Continually pinch stem tips to stimulate branching and compact growth. Under these conditions, fragrant knotweed becomes a thick, dense, attractive plant that can be used along borders and as a filler plant to offset other herbs.

PESTS: Grasshoppers chew the leaves. Hand removal is the best control.

COMMENTS: Grows rapidly.

Solanum torvum Swartz
Solanaceae, the nightshade family

COMMON NAMES: English: nightshade, turkeyberry, pea aubergine; Okinawan Japanese: *seiban nasubi;* Pilipino: *talong na ligaw, tandang-aso;* Thai: *ma khuea phuang;* Vietnamese: *ca phao.*

DESCRIPTION: Spiny shrub or tree up to 15 feet tall, woolly pubescent on all parts with stellate (star-shaped) hairs. Leaves petiolate, blade ± ovate in outline, base ± cordate, margins sinuately lobed to almost entire, apex pointed to obtuse. Inflorescences axillary, many branched, umbellate, the stalks with glandular hairs. Flowers star-shaped, < 0.5 inch in diameter, faintly fragrant, petals white, anthers bright yellow. Fruit a spherical, firm berry ca. 0.33 inch in diameter that becomes dry when fully ripe. Seeds numerous, tiny.

DISTRIBUTION: Originally native to the West Indies and now pantropical through cultivation and as a weed. *Solanum torvum* was introduced to Southeast Asia a very long time ago and today it is widely used in cuisines throughout the region. *Solanum torvum* is listed by the USDA as a federal noxious weed; therefore, growing or transporting it is prohibited. Despite this, it is being cultivated by Southeast Asian immigrants living in Hawai'i and the fruits can be found in local ethnic produce markets.

USE: The fruits are used when full sized but unripe (green) as an ingredient in Thai curries, sauces, and salads. The fruits are bitter and may be blanched in one or more changes of hot water before adding them to a curry. When used in sauces and salads, they are usually put in raw for precisely the bitter flavor they impart. The fruits are similarly used in Malaysia, Indonesia, and other parts of Southeast Asia. *Panang*-style curry from peninsular Thailand is one type of Thai curry for which *ma khuea phuang* is an essential ingredient; the watered-down version of this curry served in Thai restaurants in America bears little resemblance to the piquant authentic one, which derives a unique flavor from these small nightshade fruits.

EXPOSURE: Full sun.

PROPAGATION METHODS:

Seed: The federal noxious weed status for this species means seed is not available commercially. Locally, growers save seed from plants already growing in the garden for propagation. Seed should be sown about 1/4 inch deep, evenly distributed, covered with a loam medium, and watered to keep moist. Once the seedlings are 2 inches tall, they may be planted out. A single plant produces enough fruit for a household.

Solanum torvum

Cuttings: Not applicable.
Division: Not applicable.

CULTURAL PRACTICES: The turkeyberry requires plenty of space in which to grow, eventually developing into a gangly 12- to 15-foot-tall short-lived tree. To control the growth, pinch and prune regularly so that the fruits are within reach. Unfortunately this species can become weedy, springing up some distance from the parent plant. It is suspected that birds distribute the seed. Turkeyberry thrives in sunny, dry habitats in Hawai'i. Once the plant becomes woody, new growth does not develop readily. At this stage, replacement with a vigorous young plant is suggested.

PESTS: None observed.

COMMENTS: Very fast growing.

Tamarindus indica Linnaeus
Fabaceae (or Leguminosae), the bean family

COMMON NAMES: English: tamarind; Lao: *'kham;* Okinawan Japanese: *tama-rindo;* Pilipino: *salomagi, sampaloc;* Thai: *ma khaam;* Vietnamese: *cay me, khoua me, mak kham, me.*

DESCRIPTION: Evergreen tree up to 60 feet tall with a rounded crown of drooping branches that may almost reach the ground. Leaves alternate, even-pinnately compound, with 10–20 pairs of opposite, almost sessile, oblong leaflets. Inflorescence a terminal drooping raceme 2–4 inches long. Flowers bilaterally symmetrical, cassia-like, petals 3, about 0.5 inch long, pale yellow streaked with red; fertile stamens 3, alternating with sterile staminodes; pistil curving upward, hairy, with a small, club-shaped stigma. Fruit a brittle, curved pod, 2–6 inches long and ca. 1 inch wide, slightly flattened and scurfy brownish on the outside. Seeds 1–10, obovoid, flattened, < 0.5 inch long, embedded in a sticky, sweetish pulp through which run tough, stringy fibers.

DISTRIBUTION: Tamarind is probably native to tropical Africa, but it was introduced to India long before Europeans reached the area and now it is widespread through cultivation for its edible properties and as a shade tree.

USE: Many parts are edible: The flowers, leaves, and young fruits are cooked as vegetables; the ripe fruits are cracked for the sweetish pulp, used in curries, sauces, syrups, chutney, drinks, ice cream, jellies, and preserves. Mixed with ice it makes a refreshing beverage in Latin America. The tart pulp is integral to many kinds of curry paste in India, Thailand, and Indonesia and is also used in sour soups. A cultivar with pulp sweet enough to eat off the tree is popular in north-central Thailand. The seeds can be eaten after roasting or boiling and may be ground into flour.

EXPOSURE: Full sun.

PROPAGATION METHODS:

Seed: The large seeds remain viable for months and germinate within a week after sowing. Soaking the seed in hot water before sowing will accelerate germination. Remove all traces of fruit pulp, then place seeds in a 1-cup measure and cover with almost boiling water. Allow water to cool and let seeds soak in it for eight to twelve hours. Drain, then cover seeds 1 inch deep in loamy soil, firm the medium, and water well. When two sets of leaves have developed, the seedlings may be transplanted to individual 4-inch pots.

Cuttings: Selected cultivars of tamarind are grown in Asia by cuttings, air layers, budding, and grafting to assure that desirable characteristics are maintained. Cuttings

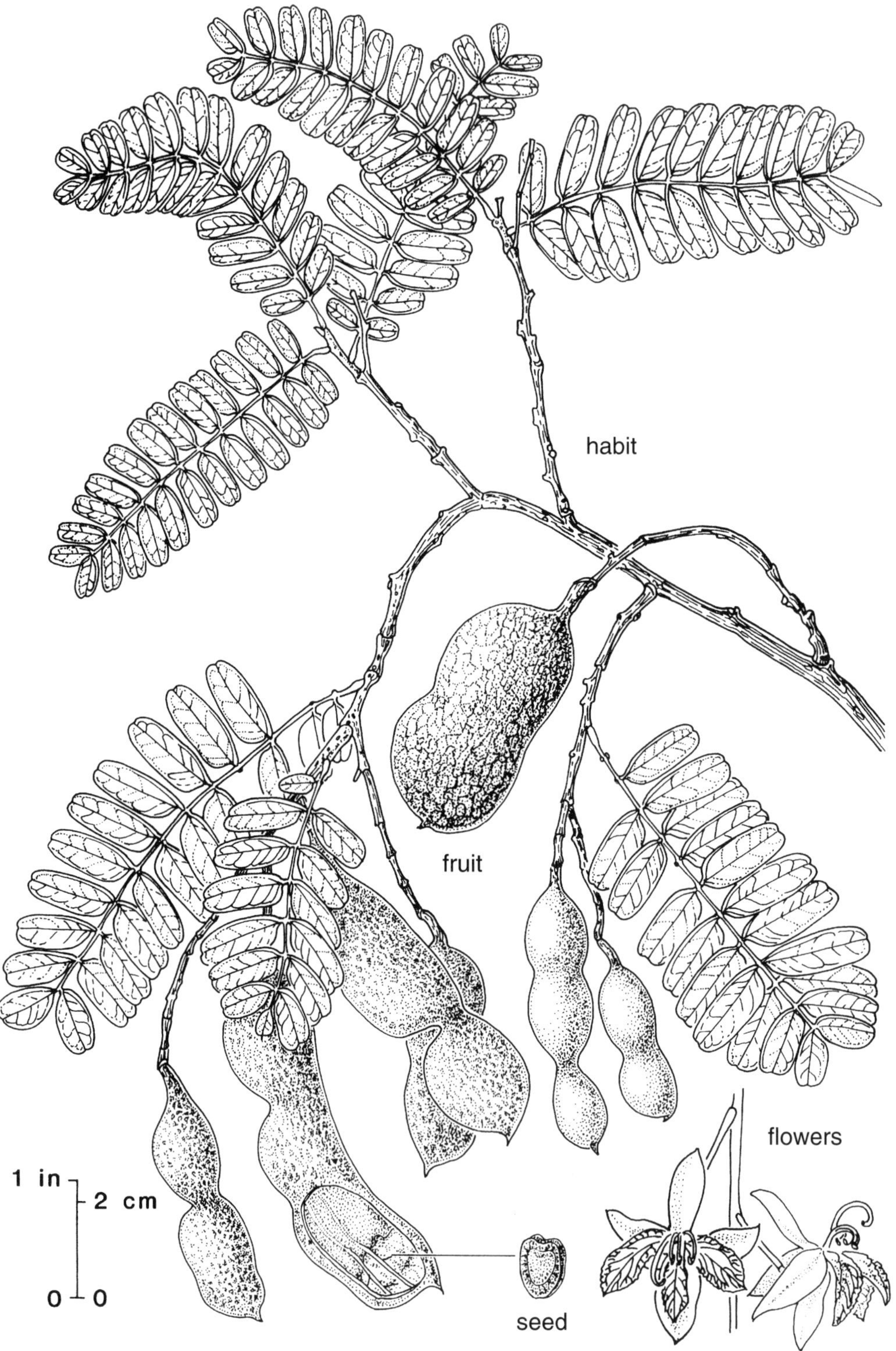

Tamarindus indica

can be rather slow to root. If cuttings are attempted, woody cuttings may be treated with a #3 rooting hormone, then inserted in a medium with bottom heat and overhead mist. Plant out only when the roots are well established. Keep shaded for a week after planting.

Grafting: Although practiced in Asia, where improved cultivars of tamarind have been selected, grafting is never practiced in home cultivation.

Air layers: From the literature, it appears that air layers work well but are time-consuming. Peel the bark from a 1-inch length of woody stem at least ½ inch in diameter. Enclose this bare area in damp sphagnum moss about 1 inch thick, then wrap in black plastic and tie the ends tightly to retain moisture. When roots are visible at the edges of the plastic wrapping, the air layer may be cut off below the layer and potted up. Keep shaded for a week or so while the roots develop.

Division: Not applicable.

CULTURAL PRACTICES: This is a low-maintenance tree that requires minimum pruning. The pale green foliage and weeping branches make this an aesthetically pleasing addition to the landscape. In time, a tamarind tree will develop a 30-foot canopy spread and grow up to 60 feet tall. Young trees should be pruned only to promote strong, balanced branch structure. Tamarind tolerates poor, stony soil, drought, and salt spray once established. Some local bonsai growers have made attractive dwarfed specimens of tamarind.

PESTS: None observed.

COMMENTS: Tamarind has a moderate rate of growth.

Zanthoxylum beechianum K. Koch

Synonym: *Zanthoxylum arnottianum* Maximowicz

Rutaceae, the citrus family

COMMON NAMES: English: prickly-ash; Okinawan *sanshō;* Japanese: *hire-sanshō;* Okinawan: *sensu, sensuru-gii.*

DESCRIPTION: A prickly, sprawling shrub tending to form a dense mound up to 3 feet tall, male and female flowers on separate plants; twigs armed with short paired spines at the base of leaves. Leaves odd-pinnately compound, 1–2.5 inches long; the main axis narrowly winged, prickly, leaflets 3–7 pairs plus a terminal leaflet, glossy, margins rolled under and nearly entire, gland-dotted. Inflorescences axillary clusters; flowers unisexual, greenish, minute (< 0.1 inch long), petals 5–7, white; male flowers with about 5 stamens; female flowers with 4 or 5 free carpels each containing 2 ovules; styles free, stigma globose. Fruits clusters of 1–5 dehiscing capsules, each ca. 0.15 inch diameter, 1-seeded. Seeds round and shiny black.

DISTRIBUTION: Native to Okinawa and the Bonin (Ogasawara) Islands, where it is commonly found growing near the sea, often on sandy or limestone soils; it also grows inland in the hills. Field collectors have noted that house flies are attracted to the plants when in flower and will gather in large numbers on the foliage and blooms.

USE: This Okinawan species is used in Hawai'i in the same way as true Japanese *sanshō*, derived from *Zanthoxylum piperitum* (Linnaeus) de Candolle, a temperate zone species that does not thrive in our climate except at higher elevations. The dried whole fruits and seeds are ground up, together or separately, or combined with black pepper. (A shaker of *sanshō* powder is often placed as a condiment on the tables in a Japanese restaurant.) The young leaves are boiled together with meat or fish to suppress strong odors and are sometimes put in soups or other dishes to enhance their flavor. A special cake called *kiri-sanshō* is made from the roasted, ground fruits, and seeds are kneaded into flour as a flavoring.

In Chinese cuisine, the seeds and fruits of *Z. piperitum* and *Z. bungei* Planchon are the "Sichuan peppercorns" that give many dishes from western Chinese provinces their distinctive flavor; they are toasted whole, then ground in a mortar and pestle before use.

EXPOSURE: Full sun.

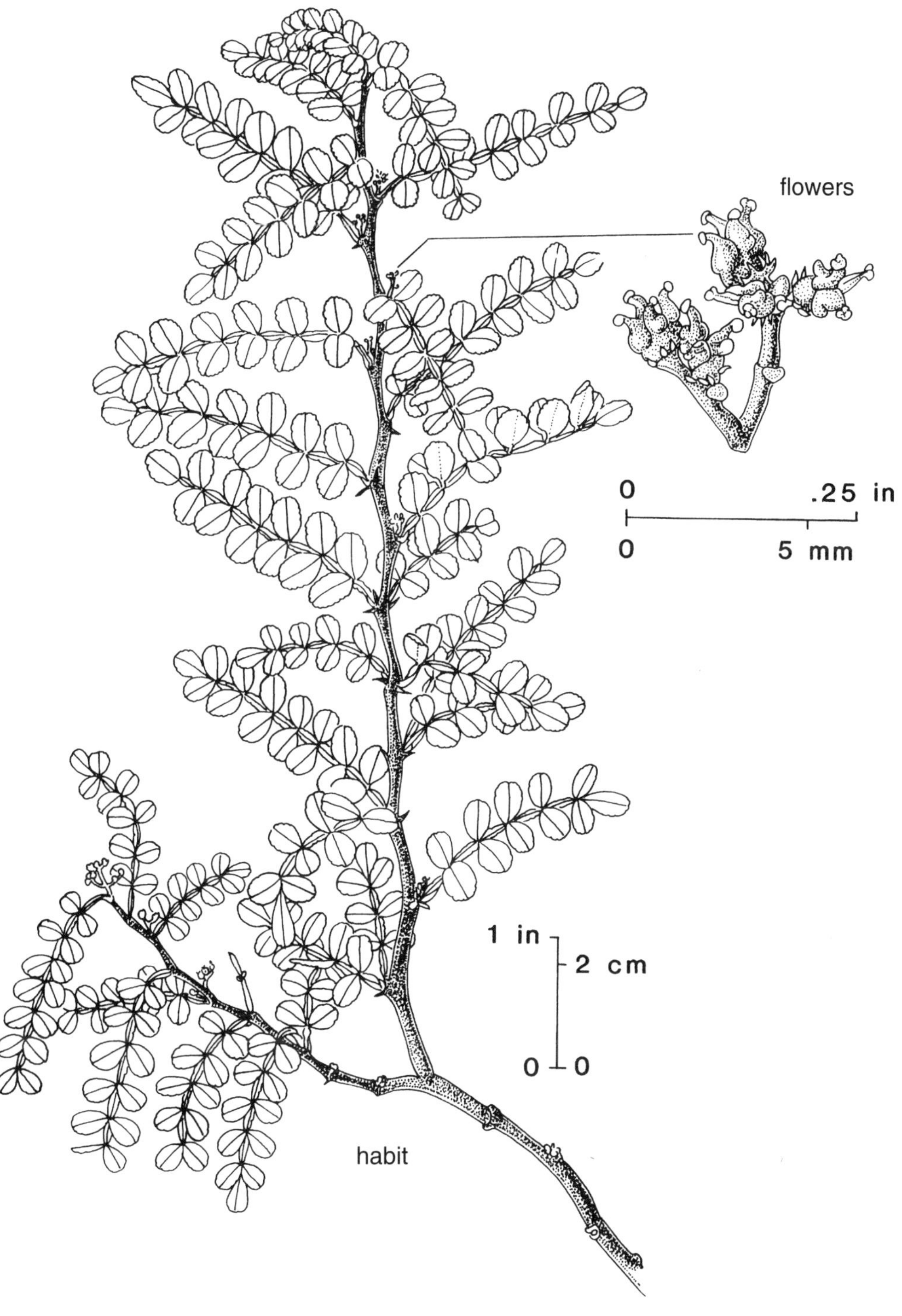

Zanthoxylum beechianum

PROPAGATION METHODS:

Seed: Plants grown in Hawai'i seem to produce only flowers of one sex and seed has not been observed to form.

Cuttings: Stem cuttings 2.5–3 inches long are taken during the cooler months. Prepare them by removing the leaves from the lower two-thirds of each cutting. Dust the leafless part of each cutting with #1 rooting hormone powder, then insert into a medium of 50:50 thoroughly washed sand-peat moss; this medium should be dense. Water thoroughly and keep damp. Overhead mist and bottom heat improve the efficacy of root formation.

With *Z. piperitum* grown in temperate climates, root cuttings may be made in winter while the plants are dormant and treated the same as for stem cuttings. It is unknown whether this method works in Hawai'i for *Z. beechianum.*

Air layers: This technique is adequate when only a few plants are desired, but commerical growers typically want more plants more quickly, so cuttings are preferred.

Division: Not applicable.

CULTURAL PRACTICES: Only small specimens of Okinawan *sanshō* have been seen, which leads one to suspect that it is slow growing under Hawaiian conditions. It appears to be ideally suited to containers, or it may be planted into the ground where it will eventually develop into a sprawling, mounding shrub. In the wild it grows near beaches on sandy or alkaline coral soils, and thus it would seem to be suited for salt spray exposure, full sun, and drying winds. A sharply drained medium is necessary. Okinawan *sanshō* benefits from pruning while the plant is young to form long, rank-looking shoots into a compact growth form that is more attractive.

PESTS: None observed.

COMMENTS: Slow growing and perhaps a plant with potential for bonsai.

Zingiber mioga (Thunberg) Roscoe
Zingiberaceae, the ginger family

COMMON NAMES: English: ginger bracts, *mioga* ginger; Japanese: *myōga;* Chinese: *keong fa, xiang he.*

DESCRIPTION: Deciduous perennial herb 1.5–3 feet tall. Leaves nearly sessile, borne in 2 ranks, blade lanceolate to narrowly oblong, 8–14 inches × 1–2.5 inches, narrowing into a short, petiole-like base. Inflorescence on a separate stalk that arises obliquely or horizontally from the rhizome, the cluster of bracts erect, ellipsoidal, 1–2.75 inches long, whitish becoming brownish. Flowers pale yellow, corolla tubular, projecting beyond the bracts, the lateral lobes whitish, the labellum with an obovate lip about 2 inches across, yellow; anthers crested, pale greenish.

DISTRIBUTION: Native to Japan, where it grows in damp woods on the islands of Honshu, Shikoku, and Kyushu; *myōga* is also cultivated in Japan and elsewhere.

USE: The flower bracts are sliced and served raw as a relish, used in soups and fried foods, or may be pickled with salt, vinegar, or sake. The blanched young leaves are used in soups and for a variety of other dishes. The inflorescences are harvested in the early stages of development or before the flowers open; the leaves are usually blanched (etiolated) before using by inverting a ceramic pot or wooden container over the plant to block out light and induce development of pale, yellowish leaves that lack chlorophyll. A variegated form is grown for its ornamental value. Because *myōga* is quite hardy, it could be grown in cooler climates than many other gingers. The lovely flowers each last only a single day, although the inflorescence as a whole may bloom for several weeks.

EXPOSURE: Partial shade in a moist, cool environment; plants do poorly in hot, sunny, dry conditions. If the growing conditions are hot and dry, the entire plant becomes ugly looking, with brown leaf margins. In Hawai'i, the most attractive specimens grow in the shelter of larger plantings.

PROPAGATION METHODS:

Seed: Not applicable.

Cuttings: Cuttings of rhizomes (modified stems) 4–6 inches long will rapidly generate roots and send up new shoots. Plant in a rich organic soil so the rhizome is covered 1 inch deep. Water thoroughly after planting and water again only when new growth is visible. Once the root system has established itself, the cuttings can be lifted from the propagating medium and planted out in the final planting bed.

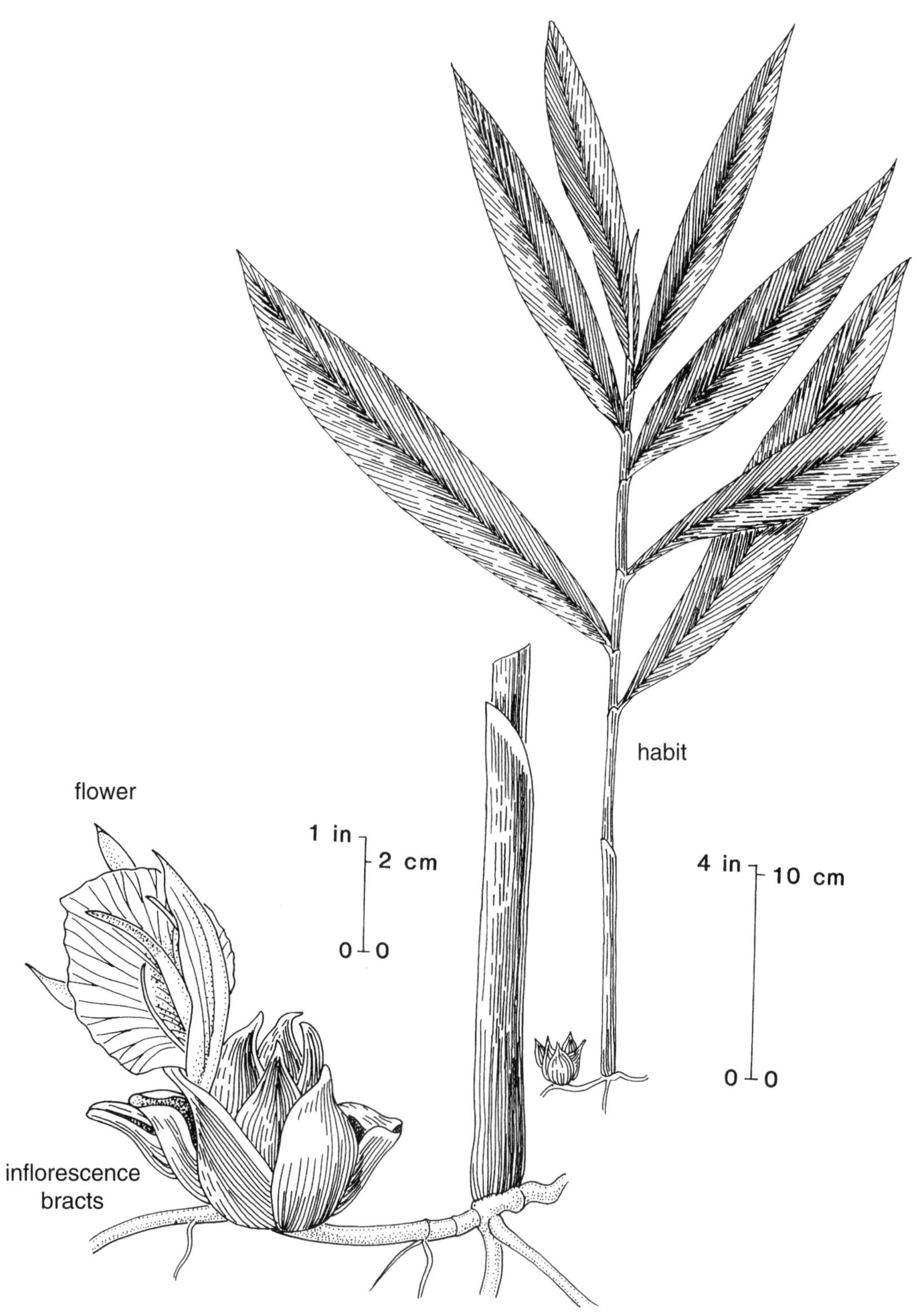

Zingiber mioga

Division: Mature plants can be divided by lifting the clump with a spading fork and cutting through the rhizomes with a sharp knife. This will be easier if the erect, above-ground stems are pruned down to within 1–2 inches of the rhizome. Divide into sections, each 6–8 inches long, discarding the older parts (rear portions of rhizome) and retaining vigorous young rhizomes near the actively growing tips. It is best to prune the roots to 6 inches in length before replanting. Set the rhizome sections 2 inches deep in well-dug, organically enriched soil and water well. Do not water again until new growth emerges, then water regularly as the developing plants require.

CULTURAL PRACTICES: Like most gingers, *myōga* grows best in a rich organic soil with good drainage. The rhizomes will fill the growing space in a few years, after which the entire clump can be dug up, divided, and then replanted. This is best done during the winter months when the plants are dormant. At the time of replanting, the soil is best dug to a depth of 12–18 inches and renewed with an addition of one-third humus. This should be thoroughly mixed and rhizome sections 6–8 inches long replanted; allow 12 inches square for each section. Water throughly after planting, then water only as the new growths start to emerge above ground level. If this replanting is done early in the dormancy, the soil can be left to nearly dry out before rewatering. In the tropics, however, the plants are often transplanted during active growth, which sets the plants back and results in a loss of the crop for that season. Active growth begins in late spring (April, May) and flowering occurs between July and October; after flowering ceases the plants die down to ground level and remain dormant until the next year.

PESTS: None observed.

COMMENTS: Grows rapidly. Mature plants with plump rhizomes planted during dormancy will rapidly develop. The second season after planting usually produces an improved crop. *Myōga* tolerates lower temperatures than do most members of the ginger family and has potential as an ornamental for temperate areas of the United States.

Zingiber officinale Roscoe
Zingiberaceae, the ginger family

COMMON NAMES: English: ginger, ginger root; Chinese: *geung, jiang, keong;* Japanese: *shōga;* Korean: *saeng gang;* Okinawan: *sōgā;* Pilipino: *laya, luya;* Thai: *khing, khing khlaeng;* Vietnamese: *cay gung, gung.*

DESCRIPTION: Slender perennial herb arising from a stout, horizontal, palmately branched rhizome; roots fibrous, in surface layers of soil. Stems few per rhizome, 1 to 3 feet tall, erect. Leaves in 2 ranks, blade almost sessile, linear-lanceolate, 2–10 inches × 0.25–1.25 inches, tapering to a slender tip. Inflorescence borne on a separate leafless stalk about 4–8 inches tall, a pine cone-shaped head of densely overlapping bracts, 1.25–3 inches long and 0.5–1 inch wide; bracts green with a pale margin, sometimes turning reddish. Flowers 1 per bract, short lived, the corolla tube about 1 inch long, the corolla lobes yellowish, the labellum 0.5 inch wide, dull purple with cream blotches at base. Fruits very rarely produced, a thin-walled, 3-celled capsule. Seeds small, black, arillate.

DISTRIBUTION: Ginger is unknown in the wild state and seems to have been cultivated in tropical Asia since antiquity. Perhaps its wild ancestor originated in India or southern China, two countries where it has been grown since before written records were kept. Ginger is grown commercially today in China, Taiwan, Jamaica, Mauritius, several West African countries, Uganda, Fiji, Tonga, Hawai'i, and northern Queensland, Australia.

USE: The use of fresh ginger rhizome in cooking is an ancient practice in Asian cooking that has only recently gained favor in the United States. Much of the supply for the West Coast of the mainland originates in Hawai'i; the East Coast supply comes from Jamaica and, to a lesser extent, southern Florida. Fresh ginger is used to brew ginger beer and ginger ale. Traditionally the dried, ground rhizome is the ginger used in baking. Dried ginger comes from diverse sources: Africa, Jamaica, and India all contribute to the world supply. Of minor importance are crystallized and preserved ginger, most of which is manufactured in Hong Kong. Depending upon the technique used, these sugar-treated products are eaten as a confection or used in Chinese, Thai, and other Asian cuisines to add color and piquancy to certain dishes.

EXPOSURE: Partial protection from sun and full protection from drying winds are advisable. Ginger will survive in full sun if given abundant water, but plants will be shorter and apt to have brown leaf margins. When grown commercially, ginger is often interplanted with crops such as pigeon pea, castor bean, or yams that provide shade and serve as windbreaks.

PROPAGATION METHODS:

(Note: Rhizomes purchased in the supermarket can be used to start a ginger plant. Select firm rhizomes with no trace of shriveling, breaks, or mold on the skin. The ends

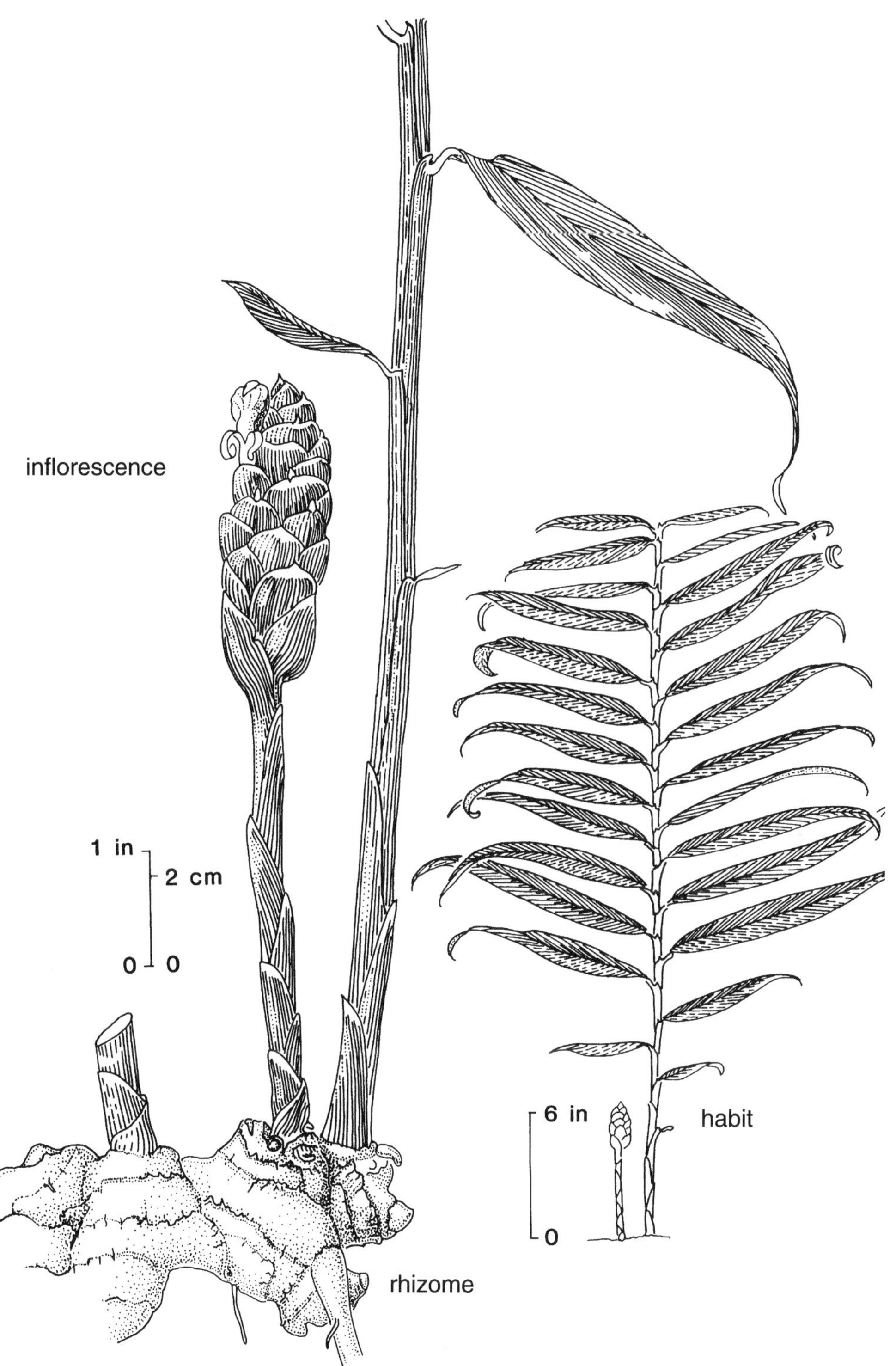

Zingiber officinale

of the fingerlike rhizome branches should be bluntly pointed and undamaged; the "eyes" contained in the points are where new stems will develop. Follow the instructions for Division, below.)

Seed: Seed is rarely produced and this method is not used in Hawai'i.

Cuttings: Rhizome cuttings are rarely used because division is so common. A clump of plants can be lifted with a spading fork and completely cleaned of roots and soil. Cut rhizomes into 3- to 4-inch lengths, remove old roots, and cut back aerial stems to 2 inches long, then insert in a 50:50 peat-perlite mix. Cover rhizome to its own thickness, water thoroughly, and do not water again until the new shoot emerges. New roots will develop quickly and dormant nodes will sprout. After the cuttings are well rooted, remove from the rooting medium and plant out into a shaded location.

Division: By far the most common means of propagation in Hawai'i. The best time to divide clumps of plants is when the aerial stems have died back to ground level, usually in the winter months. Cut off the old aerial stems that have yellowed to a length of 2 inches and lift the entire clump of plants with a spading fork, damaging the rhizomes as little as possible in the process. Wash the soil away from the root mass and then use a sharp knife to cut the rhizome into 4- to 6-inch lengths. Longer rhizome pieces will produce a larger plant in a shorter time. Discard the old rhizomes from the rear end (farthest away from the youngest aerial stems) and trim the roots to 6 inches or less to make replanting easier. If replanting cannot be completed immediately, cover the rhizomes with damp cloth or newspaper and keep protected from drying sun and winds.

CULTURAL PRACTICES: Ginger develops rapidly in humid tropical and subtropical climates, particularly on rich organic loam soils. Prepare the soil by digging to a depth of 12–18 inches and adding one-third rich organic humus. Plant rhizomes 12 inches apart and 1–2 inches below the surface. Firm soil over the rhizomes and water thoroughly. Water sparingly or not at all until the new shoots emerge above the soil, then increase watering so the new shoots do not dry out.

As the ginger plant finishes flowering, the leaves will turn first yellow, then brown. The old stems are best cut down to ground level and watering tapered off during the dormant season. Thinning improves air circulation and provides space for the new shoots that will emerge in the next growing season. Mature plants can be thinned out annually by removing old tattered stalks and leaving developing stems. This keeps plants looking tidy and allows the flower spikes to be more easily observed. In hot sun, the leaves develop a pink tinge before margins turn brown. For established plants not requiring division, a top dressing of organic mulch may be added during dormancy. Apply fertilizer at the beginning of the growing season as stems emerge, and water thoroughly.

PESTS: Leaf margins are chewed by nocturnal insects of an unknown type.

COMMENTS: Rapid growing once established. Growth appears slow during the first year, but after establishment the plants multiply rapidly. Division is recommended when aerial stems become densely crowded. This indicates that the underground rhizomes are also crowded, which has to be alleviated promptly lest the quality of the rhizomes deteriorates.

Appendix A: Herbs Grouped by Botanical Families

Following is a list of herbs treated in this book grouped by botanical families.

Apiaceae: *Coriandrum sativum, Cryptotaenia canadensis, Eryngium foetidum*

Asteraceae: *Artemisia vulgaris, Chrysanthemum coronarium*

Compositae: *see* Asteraceae

Fabaceae: *Tamarindus indica*

Gramineae: *see* Poaceae

Labiatae: *see* Lamiaceae

Lamiaceae: *Mentha (aquatica, Ocimum basilicum, Ocimum tenuiflorum, Perilla frutescens, Plectranthus amboinicus*

Leguminosae: *see* Fabaceae

Liliaceae: *Allium tuberosum, Hemerocallis* sp.

Moringaceae: *Moringa oleifera*

Pandanaceae: *Pandanus amaryllifolius*

Piperaceae: *Peperomia pellucida, Piper lolot*

Poaceae: *Cymbopogon citratus*

Polygonaceae: *Polygonum odoratum*

Rutaceae: *Citrus hystrix, Murraya koenigii, Zanthoxylum beechianum*

Saururaceae: *Houttuynia cordata*

Scrophulariaceae: *Limnophila chinensis* subsp. *aromatica*

Solanaceae: *Capsicum annuum, Capsicum baccatum, Solanum torvum*

Umbelliferae: *see* Apiaceae

Verbenaceae: *Lippia micromera, Lippia origanoides*

Zingiberaceae: *Alpinia galanga, Boesenbergia rotunda, Curcuma longa, Elettaria cardamomum, Zingiber mioga, Zingiber officinale*

Appendix B: Honolulu Community Gardens Program

This program occupies ten sites around the island of O'ahu. The site locations and the number of plots in each garden are provided for those who wish to visit these fascinating cross-sections of home gardening as practiced in Hawai'i.

Ala Wai Community Garden
Located at the end of University Ave. between Ala Wai Elementary School and the Ala Wai Canal; 155 plots 12 feet × 15 feet.

Diamond Head Community Garden
Located between Pākī and Lē'ahi Avenues at the base of Diamond Head, adjoining Kapi'olani Park; 110 plots 5 feet × 17 feet.

Dole Community Garden
Located at the end of Frear Street (enter from Magellan Street); 27 plots 10 feet × 10 feet.

Foster Community Garden
Located in Foster Botanical Garden behind the Kuan Yin Temple; 60 plots 5 feet × 20 feet.

Hawai'i Kai Community Garden
Located on Maniniholo Street off Lunalilo Home Road; 40 plots 10 feet × 10 feet.

Kāne'ohe Community Garden
Located on Puhuwai Place, off Kea'ahala Road; 33 plots 10 feet × 10 feet.

Makiki Community Garden
Located in Makiki District Park off Makiki Street near St. Clement's Church; 160 plots 10 feet × 10 feet.

Honolulu Community Gardens Program

Mānoa Community Garden
Located next to Mānoa Elementary School on Kahaloa Drive (enter from Mānoa Road or East Mānoa Road; 98 plots 10 feet × 20 feet.

Mō'ili'ili Community Garden
Located between Isenberg and Coolidge Streets; 68 plots 10 feet × 10 feet.

Wahiawā Community Garden
Located at the corner of Kamehameha Highway and Military Road, across from Wheeler Army Air Field; 465 plots 20 feet × 40 feet.

Annotated Bibliography

Andrews, J. *Peppers: The Domesticated Capsicums.* Ed. 2. Austin: University of Texas Press, 1995. [The definitive reference on chili peppers.]

Blackmore, S. *Penguin Dictionary of Botany.* Middlesex, England: Penguin, 1984. [General reference for botanical and horticultural terms.]

Bonk, S. K. F. *The Farmers Market Is Cookin'.* Hilo: Hilo Bay Printing, 1993. [Local recipes from Hawai'i's diverse ethnic mix collected from growers and vendors in the Hilo Farmers Market.]

Bown, D. *The Encyclopedia of Herbs and Their Uses.* New York: Dorling Kindersley, 1995. [A lavishly illustrated and comprehensive work on herbs of all types.]

Brickell, C. *The Encyclopedia of Gardening Techniques.* New York: Exeter Books, 1984. [General reference for horticultural practices.]

Burkill, I. H. *A Dictionary of the Economic Products of the Malay Peninsula.* 2 vols. Kuala Lumpur: Governments of Malaysia and Singapore, Ministry of Agriculture and Co-operatives, 1966. [Encyclopedic reference on useful plant and animal products of Malaysia.]

Chung, H. L., and J. C. Ripperton. *Utilization and Composition of Oriental Vegetables in Hawaii.* Honolulu: Hawaii Agricultural Experiment Station Bulletin 60, 1929. [An outstanding reference on Chinese and Japanese herbs and vegetables grown in Hawai'i; now out of print.]

Codd, L. E. "*Plectranthus* (Labiatae) and Allied Genera in Southern Africa." *Bothalia* 11 (4): 371–442 (1975). [Taxonomy of *P. amboinicus* and its origin in Africa.]

Cook, A. D., ed. "Oriental Herbs and Vegetables: A Handbook." *Plants & Gardens* 39 (2): 1–76 (1983). [Excellent handbook with articles about Chinese, Japanese, and Thai culinary and medicinal herbs.]

Cost, B. *Bruce Cost's Asian Ingredients.* New York: William Morrow, 1988. [A cookbook with a well-researched introductory chapter on Asian herbs.]

Cramer, L. H. "Lamiaceae." In *A Revised Handbook to the Flora of Ceylon,* ed. by M. D. Dassanayake and F. R. Fosberg, vol. 3: 108–194. New Delhi: Amerind, 1981. [Botanical account of mints grown and used in Sri Lanka, especially useful for *Ocimum.*]

Dahlen, M., and K. Phillipps. *A Popular Guide to Chinese Vegetables.* New York: Crown, 1983. [A well-illustrated cookbook that provides an appendix of botanical names, as well as the Chinese names in characters and Roman script.]

Everett, T. H. *The New York Botanical Garden Illustrated Encyclopedia of Horticulture.* 10 vols. New York: Garland, 1981–1982. [Encyclopedic work on plants cultivated in North America; provides horticultural information for some of the more widely available species of exotic herbs.]

Facciola, S. *Cornucopia: A Source Book of Edible Plants.* Vista, CA: Kampong Publications, 1990. [Remarkably thorough single-volume account of edible plants in the United States and Canada, with lists of cultivars, sources for seeds, and references consulted; simply jam-packed with information.]

Fernald, M. L. *Gray's Manual of Botany.* 8th ed. Portland, OR: Dioscorides Press, 1950. [Distribution in North America for *Cryptotaenia.*]

Hale, W. G., and J. P. Margham. *The Harper-Collins Dictionary: Biology.* New York: Harper-Collins, 1991. [General reference for biological terms.]

Hampstead, M. "Basil." *The Herb Companion* June/July 1989: 20–25. [Herb magazine article describing basil cultivars in the United States.]

Hartmann, H. T., and D. E. Kester. *Plant Propagation, Principles and Practices.* Englewood Cliffs, NJ: Prentice-Hall, 1983. [A standard college-level text.]

Herklots, G. A. C. *Vegetables in South-East Asia.* New York: Hafner Press, 1972. [A classic reference on useful plants of the region, it includes many herbs; has Chinese characters and phonetic transliterations.]

Howard, R. A. *Flora of the Lesser Antilles, Leeward and Windward Islands.* Vol. 4. Jamaica Plain, MA: Arnold Arboretum, 1988. [Botanical account of *Peperomia pellucida.*]

———. *Flora of the Lesser Antilles, Leeward and Windward Islands.* Vol. 6. Jamaica Plain, MA: Arnold Arboretum, 1989. [Botanical account of *Eryngium foetidum.*]

Huxley, A. J., editor-in-chief. *The New Royal Horticultural Society Dictionary of Gardening.* 4 vols. New York: Stockton Press, 1992. [Comprehensive reference for identification and basic horticultural information.]

Jacquat, C. *Plants from the Markets of Thailand.* Bangkok: D.K. Book House, 1990. [Now out of print, this field guide to the edible and useful plants found in markets in Thailand is beautifully illustrated with color photos.]

Kowalchik, C., and W. H. Hylton. *Rodale's Illustrated Encyclopedia of Herbs.* Emaus, PA: Rodale Press, 1987.[A basic organic techniques reference.]

Krahulik, J. L., and W. L. Theobald. "Apiaceae." In *A Revised Handbook to the Flora of Ceylon,* ed. By M. D. Dassanayake and F. R. Fosberg, vol. 3: 479–499. New Delhi: Amerind, 1981. [Botanical account of the parsley family in Sri Lanka.]

Kuebel, K. R., and A. O. Tucker. "Vietnamese Culinary Herbs in the United States." *Economic Botany* 42 (3): 413–419 (1988). [Describes and gives Vietnamese common names for some herbs used by the expatriate Vietnamese communities in the United States.]

L. H. Bailey Hortorium. *Hortus Third.* New York: Macmillan, 1976. [Widely consulted though out-of-date reference for identifying cultivated plants of North America.]

Larkcom, J. *Oriental Vegetables.* New York: Kodansha International, 1991. [Includes culinary herbs from Japan and China, with a handy table cross-referencing common names in these languages with their characters and the scientific names.]

Lecomte, H. *Flore Générale de l'Indo-Chine.* 7 vols. + supplement. Paris: Masson & Cie., 1907–1944. [French-language flora for Vietnam, Laos, and Cambodia with many vernacular names and full botanical descriptions.]

Liu, T.-S., and H.-C. Wang. "Saururaceae." In *Flora of Taiwan,* vol. 2, 552–555. Taipei: Epoch. 1976. [Botanical account that describes and provides uses for *Houttuynia.*]

Mabberley, D. J. *The Plant-Book.* Edition 2. New York: Cambridge University Press, 1997. [Indispensable single-volume dictionary of plant families and genera with much valuable economic botany information and cross-references by common names.]

Macdonald, B. *Practical Woody Plant Propagation for Nursery Growers.* Portland, OR: Timber Press, 1986. [In-depth reference.]

McClure, S. *Companion Planting.* Emaus, PA: Rodale Press, 1994. [Theory and practice for companion planting.]

Moldenke, H. N. "Materials toward a Monograph of the Genus *Lippia,* V." *Phytologia* 12 (5): 252–312 (1965). [Taxonomic descriptions and synonymy for *Lippia.*]

Moore, H. E. "The Cultivated Alliums, II." *Baileya* 2 (4): 117–123 (1955). [Sorts out the scientific nomenclature for and describes several common species of *Allium.*]

Morton, J. F. *Atlas of Medicinal Plants of Middle America, Bahamas to Yucatan.* Springfield, IL: Charles C. Thomas, 1981. [Vast compilation about medicinal plants from Central America; includes both culinary and poisonous species and an extensive bibliography.]

———. *Fruits of Warm Climates.* Miami, FL: Published by the author, 1987. [Vast compilation about tropical fruits; extensive bibliography.]

Norman, J. *The Complete Book of Spices.* New York: Viking Studio Books, 1991.

Ohwi, J. *Flora of Japan (in English).* Washington: Smithsonian Institution, 1984. [Botanical descriptions and distributions for several Japanese species.]

Perry, L. M. *Medicinal Plants of East and Southeast Asia: Attributed Properties and Uses.* Cambridge: MIT Press, 1980. [Medicinal uses and toxic properties for thousands of East Asian plant species.]

Philcox, D. "A Revision of the Genus *Limnophila* R. Br. (Scrophulariaceae)." *Kew Bulletin* 24: 101–170 (1970). [Taxonomy, description, distribution, and uses for *Limnophila.*]

Press, J. R., and V. V. Sivarajan. "The Application of Some Names of *Ocimum* and *Geniospora* (Labiatae)." *Bulletin of the British Museum of Natural History (Botany)* 19: 113–116 (1989). [Taxonomy of *Ocimum tenuiflorum*, formerly known as *O. sanctum.*]

Purseglove, J. W. *Tropical Crops: Dicotyledons.* Harlow, U.K.: Longman Group, 1968. [A treasure trove of information on economically important dicots.]

———. *Tropical Crops: Monocotyledons.* Harlow, U.K.: Longman Group, 1972. [A treasure trove of information on economically important monocots.]

Quisumbing, E. *Medicinal Plants of the Philippines.* Quezon City: Katha Publishing and JMC Press, 1978. [Extensive compilation on medicinal plants that contains much useful information on edible plants and chemical constituents, as well as many vernacular names in Philippine dialects and languages.]

Richards, B. W., and A. Kaneko. *Japanese Plants: Know Them and Use Them.* Tokyo: Shufunotomo, 1988. [Handbook on ornamental and edible Japanese plants, illustrated with color photos.]

Rosengarten, F., Jr. *The Book of Spices.* Revised and abridged edition. New York: Jove, 1973. [A fascinating look at the botany, history, uses, and economic import of spices.]

Saville, C. *Exotic Herbs.* New York: Henry Holt, 1997.

Smitinand, T. *Thai Plant Names: Botanical Names, Vernacular Names.* Bangkok: Funny Publ., 1980. [Compilation of Thai and Laotian vernacular names.]

Stearn, W. T. "Notes on the Genus *Allium* in the Old World." *Herbertia* 11: 11–34 (1944). [Scientific descriptions and background information on *Allium.*]

Steenis, C. G. G. J. van. "Saururaceae." In *Flora Malesiana,* series 1, vol. 3, 47–48. Djarkata: Noordhoff-Kolff, 1949. [Botanical description, distribution, and uses for *Houttuynia.*]

———. "Moringaceae." In *Flora Malesiana,* series 1, vol. 3, 45–46. Djarkata: Noordhoff-Kolff, 1949. [Botanical description, distribution, and uses for *Moringa.*]

Stone, B. C. "Studies in the Malesian Pandanaceae 27: On the Taxonomy of *'Pandan Wangi,'* a *Pandanus* Cultivar with Scented Leaves." *Economic Botany* 32: 285–293 (1978). [Botanical description, distribution, and uses for *Pandanus amaryllifolius.*]

Stuart, M., ed. *The Encyclopedia of Herbs and Herbalism.* New York: Crescent Books, 1979. [Includes some herb species covered in the present volume.]

Swingle, W. T. *The Botany of* Citrus *and Its Wild Relatives of the Orange Subfamily: Family Rutaceae, Subfamily Aurantioideae.* Berkeley: University of California Press, 1943. [Botanical description, distribution, and uses for *Citrus.*]

Uphof, J. C. Th. *Dictionary of Economic Plants.* 2nd ed. New York: Cramer, 1968. [Packed with information about economically useful plants.]

Vaughan, J. G., and C. Geissler. *The New Oxford Book of Food Plants.* New York: Oxford University Press, 1997. [A thoroughly revised and lavishly illustrated reference on food plants, including two chapters on spices and herbs.]

Wagner, W. L., D. R. Herbst, and S. H. Sohmer. *Manual of the Flowering Plants of Hawai'i.* 2 vols. Honolulu: University of Hawai'i Press and Bishop Museum Press, 1990. [Records of plants that have escaped cultivation to become weeds in Hawai'i, such as *Artemisia, Cryptotaenia, Ocimum,* and *Peperomia.*]

Walker, E. H. *Flora of Okinawa and the Southern Ryukyu Islands.* Washington: Smithsonian Institution Press, 1976. [Botanical account of *Zanthoxylum beechianum.*]

Wuerthner, T. "A Basil Banquet." *Herb Companion* June/July 1989: 27–29. [Describes several cultivars of *Ocimum basilicum* grown and used in the United States.]

Yamazaki, T. "Scrophulariacées." In *Flore du Cambodge, du Laos, et du Viêt-nam,* fasc. 21. Paris: Museum National d'Histoire Naturelle, 1985. [Botanical description, distribution, and uses (in French) for *Limnophila.*]

Index

References to illustrations are in **boldface**.

About the Authors

GEORGE W. STAPLES has been the botanist at Bishop Museum, Honolulu, since 1988, where he has been engaged in writing a new book about the cultivated plants of Hawai'i based on Marie C. Neal's classic *In Gardens of Hawaii.* For a time he had a plot in the Honolulu Community Gardens, which was his introduction to many of the herbs described in this book and to the cross-cultural exchanges that take place between gardeners. He is fascinated by the many ways in which people use plants and enjoys exploring the market places, nurseries, and craft fairs around Honolulu to discover yet more innovative uses for plant material. He gardens in Kailua and enjoys practicing "culinary botany"—cooking with locally grown herbs, vegetables, and fruits.

MICHAEL S. KRISTIANSEN was director of the Honolulu Botanical Gardens from 1989–1996. A professional horticulturist born in South Africa, he now gardens in California. He experimented with various propagation techniques to determine which ones were best suited for the herbs covered in this book. Landscape design is a particular interest, and he enjoys the ornamental aspects of herbs as well as their culinary uses. Michael happily explores new foods and is an accomplished chef, who, with his wife Terry, enjoys entertaining.